The Learning Cycle, The 21st Century and Millennial Learners

Who They Are and How to Teach Them

Bernice McCarthy, Ph.D.

About Learning, Incorporated
Wauconda, IL
Spring, 2012

Bernice McCarthy, CIO, About Learning, Inc.
While we are delighted that you value our materials
and find them useful, and while we enjoy sharing
our ideas and our work, we look with strong
disfavor on those who would copy and use our
materials without proper arrangements and without
regard for international law.

Book design by Mary Fran Zidron.
Illustrations by Margaret Gray Hudson.
Set in Palatino and Hiroshige Sans type.

Printed by About Learning, Incorporated.

ISBN: 978-1-929040-04-9

4MAT and 4MATION are registered trademarks
of About Learning, Inc.

This work is dedicated to all the Millennials,
especially the seventeen in my life.

Bernice McCarthy

While we should be wary of simple explanations, our goal is to render complex phenomena understandable.

Michael Fullan,[1] 1989

Essential Question for this Book

Is the Learning Cycle an ideal template for designing instruction for 21st century learners?

Introduction Page 1

This is a brief overview of our 21st century world, a world of heightened awareness and global interdependence and how these changes are producing a different kind of learner: students who are meaning-seeking, curious, hands-on, creative and have high access to information.

Chapter 1 Page 5
The 21st Century Millennial Learners

This chapter lists research on the Millennials, those persons born from 1982 on, their attributes and values, what they think is important to learn and do, what motivates them and what they need to support their learning. It describes what teachers must consider when making instructional decisions for and with them.

Chapter 2 Page 15
The Learning Cycle, Neuroscience and the Millennials

This chapter introduces the Learning Cycle, its relationship to current neuroscience and how the Cycle matches the way our brains work. I describe the brain process functions of each of the four quadrants of the Cycle and how they form the foundation for the key competencies of Communication, Critical Thinking, Collaborative Problem Solving and Creativity (the 4 Cs). I present current research on right- and left-brain modes of approaching learning through the eyes of four prestigious thinkers. I invite the reader to examine this research in light of the characteristics of our 21st century learners.

Chapter 3 Page 61
The 21st Century Curriculum: Competencies, Concepts and the Common Core

This chapter explains how instructional designs must conceptualize the big ideas as well as the standards and embed the 4 major competencies in learner outcomes. These are the **Partnership for a 21st Century**[2] competencies. They are Communication, Critical Thinking, Collaborative problem solving and Creativity. If our learners are to navigate through our rapidly changing environment where information is fluid and ubiquitous, they need to be highly skilled in all four. Their future requires them to deal with a global world where boundaries merge and blur and information is available 24/7 both on and off the planet. I explain how the 4MAT Cycle can manage this with a simple and elegant design template.

o

This chapter details how the use of The 4MAT Learning Cycle as a template produces a complete learning act that is a perfect match to the attributes of 21st Century Learners. The learning cycle is the theoretical foundation for the kind of instruction demanded by the values and characteristics of these young people. Teachers will need to make major paradigm shifts to manage this kind of teaching. They will be coaching more, facilitating more, leading students to self-discovery more. They will need to design their course strategies and techniques under the "umbrella" of concepts couched in these four competencies while clustering common core standards and/or their state and district standards into concepts that connect to their students. This chapter assists teachers in doing these instructional design tasks.

Chapter 5   Page 143
Assessing Around the Learning Cycle

This chapter describes in detail how to assess around the Learning Cycle. Assessment is a conversation. It is about sitting beside and judging together. It is about the value question, Why? It is about the knowledge question, What? It is about the skill question, How? And it is about the adaptation question, If? The Millennials live in the Why? and the If? Current schooling lives in the What? and the How? The 4MAT way of teaching requires new assessment techniques and practices. All strategies must lead to life-long learning. In addition, this chapter illustrates two kinds of assessment: the formative, On-the-Way assessment and the summative, At-the-Gate assessment, and how to maintain the balance of both.

Chapter 6							Page 175
The Endurance and Continuity of the Learning Cycle

This chapter briefly details the background of the Cycle. The Learning Cycle is not new. It encompasses the work of Lev Vygotsky, John Dewey, Kurt Lewin, Jean Piaget, Michael Polanyi, Alfred North Whitehead, David Kolb and Peter Senge, a time span from 1947 to the present; and includes my work with the 4MAT Model. Its value has withstood the test of time. My understanding of the simple elegance it offers teachers has convinced me that it has always been the way people learn. It has taken today's world to finally bring it to its place. This chapter chronicles its development and its usefulness in the educational sea change that is going on in the 21st century.

Acknowledgements

Ron Neif and Tom McBride for permission to use their Beloit College List for 2015 graduates. Beloit College Mind-Set List for the Class of 2015, *http://www.beloit.edu/mindset*.

*The new mission of schools is to prepare
students to work at jobs that do not yet exist,
creating ideas and solutions for products
and problems that have not yet been identified,
using technologies that have not yet been invented.*

We must teach our way out.

Linda Darling-Hammond,[3] *2010*

Introduction

The 21st Century World: Some Key Processes Shaping our Time

Curiosity is the pre-cursor to **Creativity** and our schools are filled with bored students. **Collaboration** is the key to problem solving and yet many of our students work much of their time individually. **Critical Thinking** requires understanding the conceptual structures and connections of knowledge, and yet our students are still being taught primarily content details in the obsession to raise test scores. The availability of Internet **Communication** access for creating, sharing and obtaining information has not yet been welcomed successfully into teaching as the valuable and albeit dangerous tool that it is. Yet all around us there is a palpable growing awareness of the need for these four competencies: Communication, Critical Thinking, Collaborative problem-solving and Creativity, as the foundation of a world- class education.

Today's students are living in a world undergoing a sea change; a growing awareness of the need for global networks and a deepening understanding of how everything is connected to everything else. Boundaries are disappearing, ideas are shared through social networking and monetary and financial systems are moving into closer interdependence.

> *"We are living in a global culture that must have world-wide collaboration. Nothing like this has ever happened before. Fires in Russia mean less food in Africa, nation states can no longer work alone. Our government's vertical hierarchy is the wrong structure."*

> *–Paddy Ashdown, British diplomat, High Representative for Bosnia and Heregovina, 2002-2006.*

This is the world today's learners are inheriting. It is a world of heightened awareness, with chaotic, rapid information available almost without effort, and an emphasis on deep concerns for the gap between the 1% and the rest of us. Here is a remarkable idea spoken by Queen Rania of Jordan at the Global Redesign Summit held in Doha, Qatar, May, 2010:

> *"We have an international crisis of values. The only value is human value. We need compassion, we need a currency of grace, the gold standard that every human life has value. Let us restore justice. We live in a world so interdependent that a fire anywhere threatens us all. Now is the time to confront the rising challenges of our age. There can be no economic value without human value. The key indicator of progress can be found in whether our education system works."*

Imagine a "Currency of Grace" with an education system to match!

Closer to home, the initiative of Tiffany Shlain[4] is another example of the kind of focus this generation is taking.

> *"That's the power of the social media, interdependence…When we're able to really come together around some of the biggest problems of our day with collaborative tools online and tackle some of these problems together."*
>
> —*Tiffany Shlain, founder of the Webby Awards, the Internet's most respected symbol of success. Interview on dailydot.com, 2011*

*One of the most distinctive characteristics
of the Millennials is their desire to serve.
They will represent one out of every
three adults by the year 2020.*

Bernice McCarthy, 2012

1

The 21st Century Millennial Learners

Essential Question

*What implications do the characteristics of
the 21st century learners have for the classrooms of today?*

They are confident, connected, upbeat and
open to change. They are on track to become the
most educated generation in American history.

83% of them sleep with their phones

87% share opinions online

Pew Research,[5] 2011

The most distinctive characteristics of the Millennial generation

They balance idealism with pragmatism.

They embrace social networking, believing personal contacts are more important than privacy.

They are inspired to serve the larger community.

They support racial and ethnic equality and inclusion.

They expect to improve the position of minorities, even if it means giving them preferential treatment.

They embrace change and the opportunities that come with it.

They look for win-win solutions that advance the welfare of all.

They favor a federal government that actively attempts to solve societal and economic problems.

They cite education as the second most critical issue; jobs and the economy are first.

They are tech savvy, see the Internet as a powerful force: it costs very little, removes geography as an obstacle, helps create an evolution in language and meaning with new categories of relationships.

They want blended lives with both parents fully involved in careers and family.

60% are in some form of higher education, a percentage never before attained by any other generation.

They will impact the country's religious landscape increasing its diversity and expanding the definition of what faiths are part of America's civic principles.

"This generation will become the primary force shaping America until the middle of the 21st Century…this generation will be working on major challenges for a lifetime, not just in their youth."

–Winogras and Hais,[6] *2011*

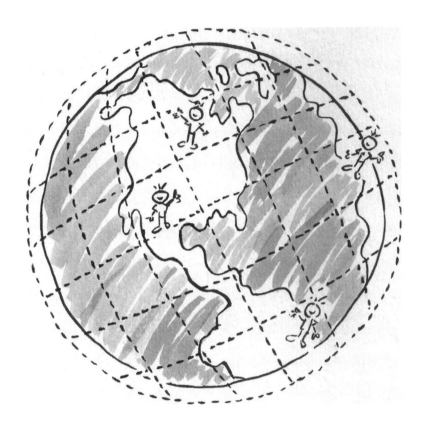

The Beloit College Mind-Set List for the Class of 2015[7]

The Beloit College Mind-Set List has been published every year since 1998. Ron Nief and Tom McBride invite us to take a look annually at the current college freshmen class. The two men have just published: *The Mindset Lists of American History* (Wiley) demonstrating how history affects mindsets of successive generations.

> The Class of 2015 is *"the symbolic generational start of a revolutionary adjustment in the systems and processes on which so much of society is built today."*
>
> –Ron Nief[8]

With the permission of the authors, I have chosen fifteen of my favorites from the seventy-five items that make up the complete list in the lives of the Class of 2015.

There has always been an Internet ramp onto the information highway.

States and Velcro parents have always required that they wear their bike helmets.

There have always been at least two women on the Supreme Court, and women have always commanded some U.S. Navy ships.

They "swipe" cards, not merchandise.

As these students have grown up on Web sites and cell phones, adult experts have constantly fretted about their alleged deficits of empathy and concentration.

Their schools' "blackboards" have always been getting smarter.

American tax forms have always been available in Spanish.

Women have never been too old to have children.

Video games have always had ratings.

Music has always been available via free downloads.

Grown-ups have always been arguing about health-care policy.

No state has ever failed to observe Martin Luther King Jr. Day.

Charter schools have always been an alternative.

They've broken up with significant others via texting, Facebook, or My Space.

They won't go near a retailer that lacks a Web site.

Altar girls have never been a big deal.

It seems the United States has always been looking for an acceptable means of capital execution.

This year's full list can be found online.

It seems likely that Millennials will be an active,
loyal and giving generation.

The point is simply this; our students
are not entirely like us.

Howe and Strauss,[9] 2007

In their book *Millennials Go To College*, Neil Howe and William Strauss discuss characteristics of 21st century learners as this group enters their senior year in college.

> *"No other adult peer group possesses anything close to their upbeat, high-achieving, team playing, and civic-minded reputation."*

The Millennials are the most racially and ethnically diverse generation in US History.

Core traits include: confidence, team-orientation, high achieving motivation, and a belief that conventional rules and standards make life work better. Howe and Strauss caution that these traits come with their own shadow sides. Team work still needs individual responsibilities. Confidence needs strong doses of humility.

Teachers must consider structure and feedback as critical for this group. They ask for team assignments, even team grading and placing more emphasis on learning that focuses on the public interest. They possess a strong incentive for stewardship. They are not content to listen to information, they have enormous access to it already. Teachers need to present and facilitate conceptual, competency-based content on real-life issues blended with cutting edge technology, complete with grading rubrics oftentimes developed with students. Remember they have grown up with Google.

Google co-founder, Larry Paige, prides the four abilities of the Google search engine: relevance, comprehensiveness, freshness and speed. This is a good illustration of what Millennials are used to:

> *Relevance: We use personalized search results based on your web history and location.*

> *Comprehensiveness: Our index is roughly 100 million gigabytes. We upgrade images, videos, news, books and more into our main search results.*

> *Freshness: We continually crawl the web minutes or even seconds after news items are posted. breaking topics from comprehensive sources just moments after events occur.*

> *Speed: Our average query response time is roughly one-fourth of a second.*

Google has a lab with 100 "shoot-for-the-stars" projects in the works. One is a space elevator anchored to earth for collecting solar system data.[10]

This makes a startling comparison to today's average classroom.

Four Key Attributes for Instructional Decisions

There are four key attributes to keep in mind regarding the best way to feel, reflect, think and act with excellence as we design instruction to educate the 21st Century Millennial Learner:

1. Their capacity for networking is all about what we can do for each other.
2. Their access to unlimited expert knowledge is enormous, speedy and multi-cultural.
3. Their commitment to stewardship is a powerful belief that obstacles, like "bugs" in software, can be fixed.
4. Their belief that we all share destinies and together can create innovative solutions with new and emerging technologies.

There are seventeen of them in my personal life. They sit in my living room and at my dining room table and talk about school. They are in elementary, high school, college and graduate school, and they talk about what they dream of, and what they want to do with their lives.

They are mostly A and B students. Here is what they say about their schooling:

"It is boring, boring, boring; tests, tests and tests, no challenges, and so little of what we are learning has very much to do with real life."

When I ask them how many great teachers they have or have had, they answer one, maybe two. The youngest one, who is ten years old, said proudly when I asked,

"I have one this year!"

What content should all our students know?
It is simply the wrong question for the 21st century, isn't it?
The real question is what competencies should we all have?

Answer the Essential Question for Chapter One

What implications do the characteristics of
the 21st century learners have for the classrooms of today?

2

The Learning Cycle, Neuroscience and the Millennials

Essential Question

*How does neuroscience add to our knowledge of
how the Learning Cycle works?*

Without biology, the learning cycle is theoretical.

*With biology, we know this is the way
the brain works.*

James Zull, 2002

In his book, *The Art of Changing the Brain*, James Zull,[11] Professor of Biology and Director of the University Center for Innovation in Teaching and Education at Case Western Reserve University, tells us the Kolb Cycle, which I refer to as "The Learning Cycle" is the way the brain works. What follows is a brief explanation of this cycle and its simple elegance and correlation with current neuroscience research.

The Learning Cycle is a simple teaching design that serves as a template to teach anyone anything. It is based on how people perceive and process information. The two points of perceiving are represented by the vertical line, and the two points of processing are represented by the horizontal line.

People tend to favor different combinations of these four points in varying degrees:

Perceiving by
Feeling and **Thinking**.

Processing by
Reflecting and **Acting**.

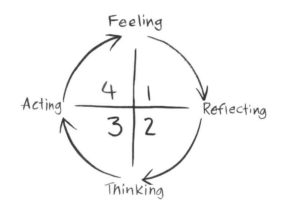

All of us do all four of these things, but we form comfort zones over time that become learning preferences, some more than others. We have a right to travel the cycle with our preferred "spin." But for real growth we need to travel the entire Cycle to complete any learning task.

The Learning Cycle, whether traveled consciously or not, is the way we learn. Any real learning does it all. And any teaching that results in learning does it all.

The Learning Cycle flows from feeling and experiencing,
to reflecting, then
to thinking and conceptualizing,
to acting, and
then moves on to a higher level of enhanced feeling and experience.
It makes sense to design learning that includes all four of these perceiving and processing points.

Type One Learners

Some of us are more comfortable in feeling our experiences and reflecting on them, yet others are more comfortable in reflecting on them and thinking about their meaning; yet others are more at home when acting on their feelings and thoughts, and the fourth group finds acting on their feelings the most preferential.

While we all favor some parts of the Cycle more than others, a complete learning act moves through all four.

The Brain Process Functions Differ in Each of the Learning Cycle Quadrants

Quadrant One: Feeling and Reflecting

Experiences activate brain neurons which create new connections.

Type One Learners
People who are most comfortable in Feeling and Reflecting

You often reflect on what is happening to you.

You come alive in your experiences.
Your brain moves from your present moment rapidly to imaging your future.

"I need to handle that when I get home," while also reflecting on the past, "I wish I hadn't said that quite that way."

You feel, then become aware of your feelings,
then you reflect on the Why?of your feelings.

You are a curious learner, open to personal honesty. You move through three stages: feeling, becoming aware of your feelings and asking yourself *why* you are having these feelings. You actively seek past connections to what you are experiencing now.

Some of us are comfortable in our feelings and reflections. And some are not so comfortable. But all of us feel and reflect. You just do these things with ease more often, and they are the essence of the communication skills of dialogue and relationship building in Quadrant One.

Type Two Learners

Quadrant Two: Reflecting and Thinking

The brain goes for the Big Idea, then fills in the details.

Type Two Learners
People who are most comfortable in Reflecting and Thinking

Your brain uses the power of images, one image leading to another.

You think about what you know as you visualize.

If it's a Big Idea, something that's important to you, you attempt to clarify it.

You relate details to it.

If intrigued by it, you critique and question it.

"What does that mean?"

" What do I need to know?"

"What will happen if I know it? If I don't?"

You are concerned with the *What?* of things, the reasons.

Some of us are comfortable in our reflections and thoughts. And some are not so comfortable. But all of us think and reflect. You just do these things with ease more often, and they are at the heart of critical thinking, the base of Quadrant Two.

Type Three Learners

Quadrant Three: Thinking and Acting

The brain loves to tinker and solve problems.

Type Three Learners
People who are most comfortable in Acting and Thinking

> You move to action when you are focused on a problem.

> You tend to see things in three dimensions setting them up in your mind as though you are ready to try a solution and see what happens.

> You enjoy tinkering and experimenting.

> You think in your doing.

> "I need to see this from all sides, not step-by-step."

> You pay great attention to immediate feedback.

> "What a minute, there may be another way." or "This not going to work this way."

> You start solving problems alone, then move into collaboration with people you respect when ready.

Some of us are comfortable in thinking while we're acting. But all of us think and act together some of the time. You just do these things with ease more often, and they are at the core of effective problem solving, the essence of Quadrant Three.

Type Four Learners

Readers can check their Learning Cycle quadrant preference
online at 4mationweb.com/4mationweb/assessment

Quadrant Four: Acting and Feeling Anew

The brain integrates and adapts where it finds meaning.

Type Four Learners
People who are most comfortable in Acting and Feeling

You tackle most tasks you deem important in an open-ended way.

You trust your gut reactions.

You tend to pass over established ways of doing things.

You keep enlarging possibilities.

This reinforces your belief you can make changes that matter in the world.

You love to push the envelope and you are very good at influencing others to do the same.

"What if we started thinking differently about this?"

"What if we tried an entirely new tack?"

You trust your ability to feel how things are going.

You honor those who keep track of details for you, so you can focus on new strategies and ideas.

Some of us are comfortable in feeling while we're acting. But all of us act on our gut feelings some of the time. You just do these things with ease more often., and these are the creativity skills of thinking "outside the box," the essence of Quadrant Four.

These four different ways of approaching learning comprise the Learning Cycle. They are the natural flow of how learning works. It makes perfect sense that learning involves feeling, reflecting, thinking and acting and moves on to new feelings and experiences.

All of these ways of being and learning are how we make meaning. None is better than any other, they are not hierarchical, they are places on the Learning Cycle that different learners favor. Robert Kegan's[12] definition of *"Learning is making meaning"* has never been trumped. We make meaning in all of these ways of being and learning. The key understanding here is the simplicity of the Cycle. We teach it in our seminars in sequence, but once mastered, it is open-ended and adaptive to whatever the teaching moment requires.

The primary mission for education can no longer be just teaching the subjects in the curriculum. It must include understanding the process of learning itself... What are the functions of the brain that are required to solve problems, think and feel about experiences, develop new theories, and determine the validity or invalidity of our thoughts, theories, and ideas?... My hope is to identify and explain how a brain becomes a mind through experience, and to create an educational agenda that will encourage and support that goal.

James E. Zull, 2002

The Learning Cycle is the process of learning itself.

The parameters of feeling, reflecting, thinking and acting call for different teaching strategies.

Each "Quadrant" focuses on a different question, from
Why do I need to know this, to
What do you want me to know, to
How does this work, and finally to
If I learn this, what will I be able to do that I cannot do now, what will I be more able to become?

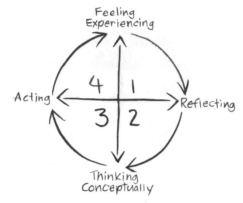

The teacher-directed, ubiquitous lecture mode does work with some of the students; it works with the Type Two Learners who focus on the "whatness" of things. They get along if the teacher is competent with the content material.

But how many of our students are Type Two Learners?

Here are a few examples from some of our research.

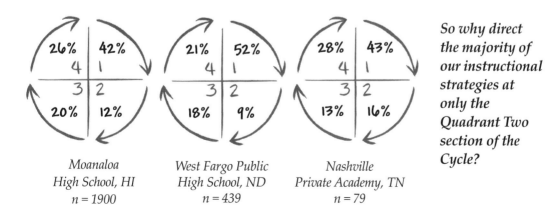

| Moanaloa High School, HI n = 1900 | West Fargo Public High School, ND n = 439 | Nashville Private Academy, TN n = 79 |

So why direct the majority of our instructional strategies at only the Quadrant Two section of the Cycle?

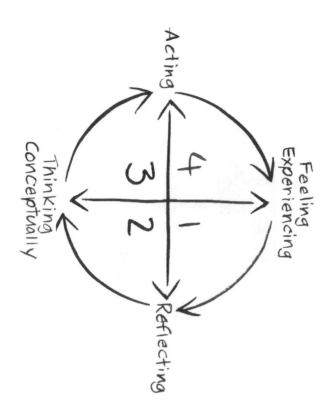

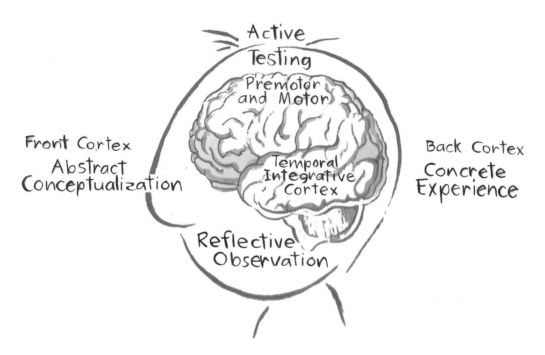

The Learning Cycle and the Zull Overlay

It turns out, the Learning Cycle and our brains work very much in the same way. Examine these two graphics, the Learning Cycle and Zull's overlay of the brain on the Cycle.

Zull takes the Learning Cycle a quarter turn, placing feeling and concrete experience on the back of the brain where the visual cortex gets input from the outside world from multiple sensory inputs.

The overlay on the Learning Cycle for reflection is at the bottom of the Cycle where the temporal integrative cortex is.

The front integrative cortex faces forward, makes decisions, plans for action, organizes activities of the body. This is our thinking, abstract conceptualizing place on the Learning Cycle.

The motor cortex that produces the movement to carry out plans is at the top of overlay on the Learning Cycle.

Zull cautions that these four functions are not absolute but true in general as different functions dominate different parts of the brain.

While both hemispheres seem to be involved in one way or another in almost everything we do, there are some very striking differences in the information-processing abilities and propensities of the two hemispheres.

Joseph Hellige,[13] 2001
(A definitive voice in this research.)

The Learning Cycle and Right-and Left-Mode Processing

In addition to Zull's belief that the Learning Cycle and our brains work basically in the same way, the important work on right- and left-mode processing originating in Roger Sperry's[14] work, is now being taken seriously.

Examine the most current research regarding these two ways of processing. A number of books by prestigious authors have taken up this issue. Following are brief descriptions from four of them.

Daniel Kahneman,[15] reports on the biases of intuition in his book, *Thinking, Fast and Slow,* what he calls the System 1 of the brain. *"We now understand the marvels as well as the flaws of intuitive thought, which is nothing more and nothing less than recognition."* He claims that System 1 influences many of our choices more than most of us realize. He calls System 1 *"Fast thinking, effortlessly originating impressions and feelings...and living much of our life guided by the these impressions."* This is what I call the Right Mode.

Whereas *"The main functions of System 2 include monitoring and controlling the thoughts and actions suggested by System 1, allowing some to be expressed directly in behavior and suppressing or modifying others."* System 2 takes over when things get demanding and we must pay attention. It regulates our self-control. He calls it Slow thinking, *"when people switch their approach to problems from a casual, intuitive mode to an engaged and analytic one."* This is what I call the Left Mode.

Chip and Dan Heath's[16] book, *Switch: How to Change Things When Change Is Hard,* is often cited in management training work.

Their book also reports on the two different brain systems, the rational mind and the emotional mind, and, in particular, how they compete for control. The Heaths have developed Jonathan Haidt's metaphor of the emotional side as the Elephant and the rational side as The Rider.

> *"Perched atop the Elephant, the Rider holds the reins and seems to be the leader. But the Elephant, our emotional and instinctive side is apt to take off on its own and there is not too much the Rider can do about it. The Elephant often looks for short term quick payoffs. The Rider's strength is the ability to think long-term."*

The Elephant's turf is love and compassion, sympathy and loyalty. The Rider's is providing the planning and direction.

Rather the balance of power has shifted where it cannot afford to go–further and further towards the part world created by the left hemisphere…and the left seems to have no awareness of its dependency on the Right, indeed it is filled with alarming self-confidence.

Iain McGilchrist

Iain McGilchrist,[17] *The Master and His Emissary: The Divided Brain and the Making of the Western World.*

He describes the functioning of the two hemispheres and their nature as two different worlds. He points out how these two sides of the brain have shaped our world. *"I believe there is a world of difference between the hemispheres. Understanding quite what that is has involved a journey through many apparently unrelated areas: not just neurology and psychology, but philosophy, literature and the arts, and even to some extent, archaeology and anthropology, and I hope specialists in these areas will forgive my trespasses."*

McGilchrist is clear on his belief regarding the fundamental difference between the two hemispheres. He maintains the difference lies *"in the type of attention they give to the world. Both are hugely valuable. They stand in opposition to one another and need to be kept apart—hence the bihemispheric structure of the brain."*

He describes the left hemisphere as having a strong concern with the *"Whatness"* of things. It yields narrow, focussed attention, sees things abstracted from context and breaks things into parts from which it then constructs a whole.

The right hemisphere is deeply involved in social functioning. It yields a broad, vigilant attention, sees things whole and in their context, forms bonds with others; i.e., empathy, emotional understandings. It outperforms left in prediction and will present an array of solutions when problem solving.

McGilchrist has strong language for the predominance of the left hemisphere in today's world. He maintains the two hemispheres need to be in balance for the harmony the world needs. Strong words. Really distressing to think of the high percentage of left-mode teaching going on in our schools!

Robert Orstein,[18] *The Right Mind: Making Sense of the Hemispheres.*

Orstein's prescient insights into the two hemispheres in 1997 revealed a picture of the differing skills of the hemispheres in an important dimension.

A patient with surgically separated hemispheres was given the task of copying three items: a rectangle, a cross and the word *"Sunday"* using first one hand then the other.

Here is how this split-brained patient performed on this task.

*left hand,
right brain*

*right hand,
left brain*

These drawings were a great personal Aha! for me. They show how the now separated right brain drew the rectangle and the other two objects and how the separated left brain fared with the same task. The right brain was able to duplicate two of the items fairly well. but not the linear word *"Sunday."* When the left brain took over, the rectangle became a series of straight lines lined up in a row, none connected to any other, unable to complete the rectangle, yet the left brain was able to successfully draw a copy of the word *"Sunday."*

As long as school testing remains so confidently
dedicated to the one right answer, the balance
needed for our learners to grow their brains
into minds is simply not there.

Bernice McCarthy, 2012

The left brain results were the source of my great Aha! The left brain could not connect the lines to form the rectangle. The right brain was able to draw the necessary connections and relationships, but was unable to copy the word *"Sunday,"* a linear task. Seeing connections and relationships is the province of the right brain and making connections is primary to all thinking.

Right: Think synthesis–resolution, forming a whole, union, fusion.
Left: Think analysis–scrutiny, investigation, dissection, elements.
Add
Right: Wonderment–eyes wide open.
Left: Concentration–eyes winced to focus.

And yet, teaching techniques and strategies continue to be filled with a dismaying number of left hemisphere tasks. As long as school testing remains so confidently dedicated to the one right answer, the balance needed for our learners to grow their brains into minds is simply not there. The methods and practices of pedagogy must include the Learning Cycle with its apt correlation to how the brain works. The Cycle encompasses best practices and can be manipulated and adapted for particular students and particular curriculum, in particular times.

When I first began working with the information on right- and left-mode processing, I could see that each of the four Learning Cycle Quadrants needed both synthesis and analysis for balanced understanding. I designed both brain processes to work in tandem with the four Cycle quadrants.

I believe insight refers to that depth of
understanding that comes by setting experiences,
yours and mine, familiar and exotic, new and old,
side by side, learning by letting them speak
to one another.

Mary Catherine Bateson,[19] 1994

The Purpose of Right- and Left- Mode Processing in the Learning Cycle

In **Quadrant One** the lesson or unit begins with an experience, something actually happens in the classroom. It follows naturally that students share their feelings and perceptions after a right-mode, concept-embedded experience. The sharing moves into analysis as comparisons are made and similarities and differences are listed or prioritized. Note how strongly the teaching strategies in Quadrant One employ a whole range of communication skills.

In **Quadrant Two,** before the left-mode teacher-directed lecture, students need to visualize the concept they have just experienced. The image is based on each student's unique reactions to the experience and perception sharing in Quadrant One. They need to do this before they begin examining the expert knowledge. Their understanding of the concept depends on their ability to image it. I added the right-mode image step to be completed before the lecture as part of the critical thinking competency of Quadrant Two.

Examine D. Frank Benson[20] on the combination of image and word to achieve high levels of understanding.

> *"The input of the two hemispheres to the overall concept appears probable. The right hemisphere is more likely to provide a visual image and the left a semantic relationship, with the combination producing the total concept. Concept formation thus appears to be a bihemispheric function with specialized input from each of the hemispheres...*
>
> *What can be stated with absolute certainty is that the two hemispheres of the human perform different functions in the use of communication symbols."*
>
> *–D. Frank Benson, 1985*

It seems a vital key to understanding and retaining important concepts to have students do both, to image the concept and master the meaning and origin of its semantic base.

In **Quadrant Three,** students need to practice the learning in the way of the experts for a solid understanding that will enable them to extend the learning into their own lives in useful and meaningful ways. First, they need to know the way of the experts. The left-mode practice in Quadrant Three is a stepping stone to extending the learning to personal adaptation, the right-mode step of Quadrant Three.

In **Quadrant Four,** the students analyze their adaptations of the learning with the help of their teacher and their peers, then integrate these adaptations into their lives.

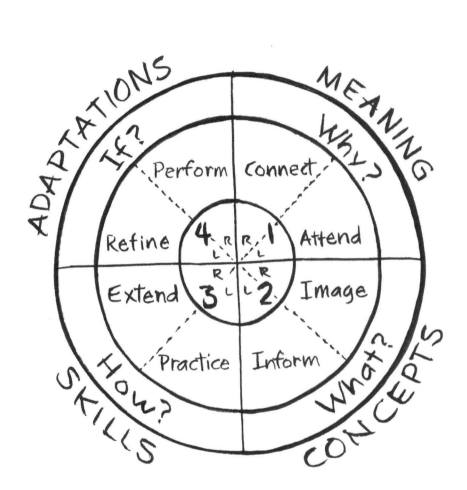

The 4MAT® Model

The eight Learning Cycle functions: right- and left-mode tasks inserted into the four quadrants.

Connect, the concept experienced

Attend, the experience shared and analyzed

Image, the concept imaged

Inform, the concept explained

Practice, the concept practiced

Extend, the personal concept adaptation planned

Refine, the adaptation analyzed, edited and honed

Perform, the conceptual learning and practice integrated

It is interesting to note that in Singapore math, the concepts are taught in steps from concrete, to pictorial, to abstract, exactly the way Quadrants One and Two of the Learning cycle work. The Singapore math[21] course emphasis is on problem solving and discovery, Learning Cycle Quadrants Three and Four. The tasks are balanced with right and left mode techniques: the children are taught model drawing (right mode) and line segment problem solving requiring sequential thinking as well as number manipulations. (left mode).

The Millennials and Right- and Left-Mode Processing

The following page is a partial list of right- and left-mode characteristics. I have drawn them from my research with the Hemispheric Mode Indicator (HMI)[17] and current neuroscience. You might find it useful to check the characteristics you are already using in your teaching.

Bernice McCarthy

Left Hemisphere	Right Hemisphere
Analysis	Synthesis
Local attention	Predominant for attention, global picture
Focuses on what it already knows	Focuses on broader, more vague things
Details	Networks
Zeros in on specifics	Unifies divided input
Starts with the pieces	Starts with the overall picture
Stays with the known	Attuned to anything novel, shifts to left after newness
Process is predictive	Process is emergent
Single solution that seems to fit	Presents an array of solutions
Abstract categories and types	Uniqueness and individuality
Grasps what has been prioritized	Dominant for exploration
Needs to do the details then	Assumes a grounding and integrating role
(Left returns to the Right's grounding after mastering the details)	
Denies discrepancies that do not fit	Attracted to discrepancies
Uses highly related words	Uses a broad array of words
Explicit meaning	Implicit meaning
Verbal	Nonverbal
Separate and objective	Emotionally engaged

Left Hemisphere	Right Hemisphere
Predictability	Possibility
Clarity	Evolving understandings
Simplifies the world	Sees the complex reality of the world
A closed system	An open system
Distinct	Nuanced
Separates	Connects
Self-referring nature of the world	On the lookout for otherness
Logical	Ironic
Serious	Humorous
Literal	Metaphoric
Clear	Ambiguous, opposites may be compatible
Isolates	Includes
Controls	Open ended
Decontextualized, labeled	Always in context
Narrow focus	Broad focus
Convinced	Changing, never fully grasped
Indifference	Empathy
Disposition toward machines	Disposition toward living things
Prioritizes the expected	Attends to the edges of awareness

Scientific theory did not seem to depend wholly on ratiocination and calculation: intuition and a sense of beauty and elegance were also important factors.

Karen Armstrong,[22] 2009

Now compare the Right and Left Hemisphere list with the characteristics of the Millennials in this overview of their traits. Put a *R* or an *L* next to their characteristics and see how your comparisons come out.

Millennial Learner Quick Overview

Need world values network   _____

See how everything connects   _____

Share ideas online voluminously   _____

Blur boundaries   _____

Have major concerns for the Earth   _____

Believe political action can make a difference   _____

Team oriented, collaboration a high priority   _____

Believe in access to all information   _____

Are inspired to service, civic minded   _____

Believe they can help restore justice   _____

Work interdependently with social media   _____

Believe in inclusion   _____

Embrace change   _____

Tech savvy   _____

Confident   _____

Optimistic and upbeat   _____

Rule followers   _____

Honor, even seek diversity   _____

It appeared that some sort of broad transfer of function was taking place between the two hemispheres from right to left throughout development, and that this transfer was not limited to language...could the two hemispheres differ between cognitive novelty and cognitive routine, with the right particularly adept at processing novel information and the left routine, familiar information?

Elkhonon Goldberg,[23] 2009

Right-mode teaching strategies attract our Millennial learners, motivating and leveraging their retention of content.

We move naturally though the Cycle from synthesis to analysis.
When we have an emotional experience, we turn inward to ponder it.
When we are introduced to a new idea, we attempt to image it.
When we are in the early stages of mastering a skill, we want to try it in ourselves.
When we master new learning, we strive to integrate it into our lives.

It's as simple as that. Synthesis and analysis, connections and separations, balance.

Examples of Teaching Strategies Requiring Both Right- and Left-mode Processing

These examples were created from some of the listed items on page 43.

Finding Both Explicit and Implicit Meaning

Explicit: stated clearly and in detail, leaving no room for doubt.

Implicit: Implied, though not plainly expressed.

The fight for equality under the law for Negroes: the Supreme Court, *Plessy v Ferguson, 1896.* The vote was clear, 7 to 1 for separate but equal facilities for white and blacks. It is one of the most infamous cases in Supreme Court history. It opened the way for Jim Crow laws to flourish. (The segregation of black people in the United States.)

The Case Particulars
The Court upheld the constitutionality of separate facilities in private businesses. like seating on railroad cars. On June 7, 1894, Homer Plessy boarded a car of the East Louisiana Railroad in New Orleans that was assigned to whites only. Plessy was considered black even though he was one-eighth black and seven-eights white and was born a free person. He refused to leave. He was arrested and jailed. He brought his case to the Supreme Court of the land and the Court ruled against him. The important issue in this case is the reasoning of the Court regarding what is explicit and implicit in this case. *(Plessy v. Ferguson, 163 U.S. 537)*

Explicit: stated clearly and in detail, leaving no room for doubt.

Implicit: implied, though not plainly expressed.

When summarizing, Justice Brown declared,

> *"We consider the underlying fallacy of the plaintiff's argument to consist in the assumption that the enforced separation of the two races stamps the colored race with a badge of inferiority. If this be so, it is not by reason of anything found in the act, but solely because the colored race chooses to put that construction upon it."*

The *Critical Thinking* required in this task asks the students to identify the explicit statement in the ruling that the state has the right to regulate railroad companies and that, according to Justice Brown, there is no discrimination of the black race involved, only in the minds of the colored race. (*"who put that construction upon it."*) The skill here is to analyze what is said, versus what is actually meant.

Therefore there was no implicit meaning involved, according to the ruling. Obviously Mr. Plessy and the *"colored race"* would vehemently disagree. This shameful law remained in place until 1964 when the Court ruled it was illegal to separate races in public places, like schools.

It could be of some consequence to have the students follow this task with an examination of the Woolworth lunch counter sit-in, February 1, 1960.

Examining Prioritized Knowledge Versus Exploratory Knowledge

Have the students examine how certain aspects of something that has been considered clearly understood could still reveal new and important insights if explored further.

Examples: pesticides still being used on human foods, the language skills of the Benobo apes, music sound decibels and possible hearing impairment, the practice of *"safe gas"* fracking to procure natural gas. All the more powerful if this task is done in *Collaborative* student groups.

Using Verbal and Nonverbal Processes to Deepen Understanding

Have primary children draw a noun and a verb in addition to memorizing verbal descriptions. Try it yourself and note the deeper understanding needed to do this task, "to draw verbness," versus knowing the definitions. What *Creative* process involved?

Our ordinary conceptual system is fundamentally metaphoric in nature.

Judith Sanders,[24] 1984

Examining Beliefs Versus Evolving Understanding

Have students examine the processes they went through when they outgrew beliefs they had as children. Have them illustrate the process metaphorically. This is an especially fine task for raising awareness of interpersonal *Communication*.

Working with Distinct Versus Nuanced Music, Art, Creative Writing

What is distinguishable in Bob Dylan's music as only Bob Dylan's music? What is nuanced? (subtle differences in shade of meaning) Or any musician they are excited about. Can they make these distinctions? Could this take a *Critical Thinking* ear?

Or a visual artist, like Wassily Kandinsky. Introduce students at any age to some of his paintings and the texts he wrote to clarify them. An excellent way to teach nuance versus distinctiveness.

Or in Creative writing have students write conversational dialogue that moves from distinct to nuanced meanings.

Note how you can insert the *4C's* into the tasks you create for your students in many fruitful ways. Grasping implicit meaning requires *Critical Thinking*; awareness of outgrowing beliefs need interpersonal *Communication*; groups working on science data require *Collaborative* problem-solving as well as *Creativity*.

The Learning Cycle and Metaphoric Thinking

Metaphors are powerful tools. If they are not an important part of your teaching, make it so. They are not just word play, they are conceptual in nature and characteristic of a high level of cognition.

Examples in Literature

The feeble blaze of life that remained in her was blown into a flame by her anxiety.

–Sherwood Anderson, Winesburg, Ohio

The black miners had watches proudly acquired as the manacles of their new slavery to shift work.

—Nadine Gorimer, *My Father Leaves Home*

The brain is a lean, mean, adaptive multitasking machine that needs proper care and feeding.

—James Zull, *The Art of Changing the Brain*, 2002

Metaphors are more tenacious than facts.

Paul de Man,[25] 1984

Neuron networks map relationships and these networks make meanings. Creating metaphors is seeing similarities in dissimilar things. This is potent brain work, both Creative and Critical Thinking.

Ask your students to create metaphors. Here are a few you might try.

The swiftness of time as one gets older

The fear of the dentist

A crowd that begins to get wild

A blinding snowstorm

An angry look from a person in charge

A field of tulips

If Frank Benson is correct that the ability to form metaphors is bihemispheric, and that it takes the combination of right and left modes to understand a concept well, then make metaphors a major part of how you teach, and a major part of how you assess as well. What better way to know if your students really understand content conceptually. Put images right into the center of your practice.

"We see that metaphors are engaging the areas of the cerebral cortex involved in sensory responses even though the metaphors are quite familiar. This result illustrates how we draw upon sensory experiences to achieve understanding of metaphorical language."

–Krish Sathian,[26] 2012

Results support a special role for the right hemisphere in processing metaphors.

Other than the two major connections between
the hemispheres, this back-front connection
is the most obvious wiring in the brain.

James Zull,[27] 2002

Understanding the Learning Cycle as it Relates to the Communication Between the Front Cortex and the Back Cortex

In addition to right- and left-mode findings there is another major connection to consider in how we learn, the back to front brain connection. The back cortex sends sensory information to the front integrative cortex and the front sends signals to the back cortex, in both images and language.

"This communication enriches our concept of experience and therefore of experiential learning, which the Learning Cycle is all about." –McCarthy[28]

The Learning Cycle and the Brain

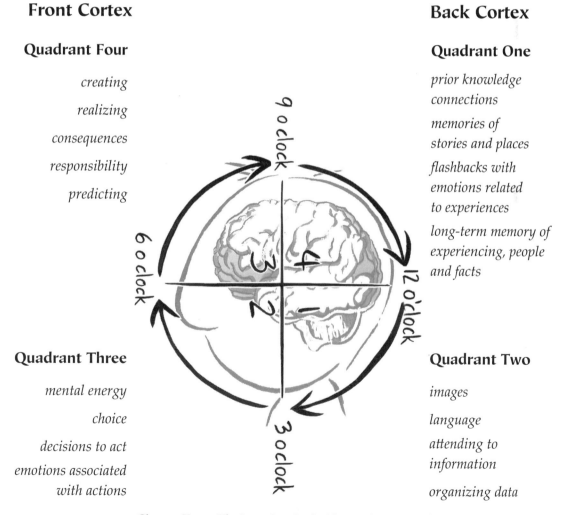

Front Cortex

Quadrant Four

creating

realizing

consequences

responsibility

predicting

Back Cortex

Quadrant One

prior knowledge connections

memories of stories and places

flashbacks with emotions related to experiences

long-term memory of experiencing, people and facts

Quadrant Three

mental energy

choice

decisions to act

emotions associated with actions

Quadrant Two

images

language

attending to information

organizing data

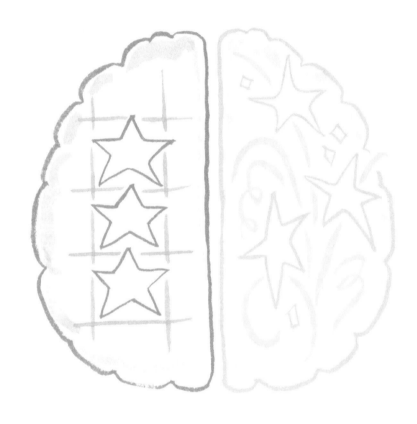

*Your brain has a capacity for learning
that is virtually limitless.*

Michael Gelb[29]

Left-Mode Processing Words

Sometimes, determining whether an activity is right-mode or left-mode can be as simple as looking at the key words. Here is a partial list of words that tend to left-mode thinking processes. *Circle the ones that are most prevalent in your teaching.*

observe	theorize	order
discuss	outline	select
diverge	test	flowchart
develop coherence	verify	write an essay
conceptualize	analyze	edit
define	write analytically	revise
classify	reason	refine
discriminate	identify	produce evidence
acquire knowledge	break into parts	verify
tell	drill	summarize
listen	uncover contradictions	assess
sit still	collect	evaluate
read	inquire	come to closure
view	predict	refocus
research	record	produce
compare	hypothesize	take a position
contrast	measure	conclude
plan	manage	form new questions

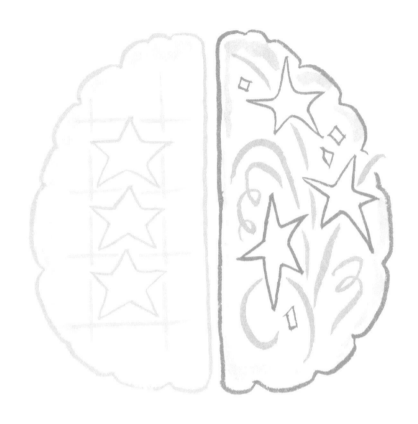

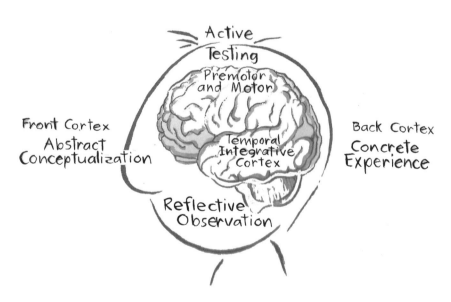

Right-Mode Processing Words

Circle the ones that you use most in your teaching.

reflect	express	tinker
relate	interact	hunch
journal	write creatively or poetically	relate to real world
brainstorm		demonstrate
visualize	pattern	synthesize
imagine	contrast	exhibit
draw	feel tone	publish
create a mindmap	feel timbre	author
associate	feel nuance	merge to a higher form
simulate	represent	integrate
role play	illustrate	create
connect	cluster	experiment

The Learning Cycle and Neuroscience: Brief Recap

Pay attention to your students' learning styles.

Use students' experiences to connect them to all new learning.

Use emotionally impacting images, stories, discussion of perceptions, all associated with sensory, decision-making and motor pathways of the brain.

Actively engage your students in hands-on tinkering, experimenting, working in teams, editing and tutoring each other. differentiating your practice options.

Move your students from hesitant practice to fluid expertise in ways they find exciting with lots of possibilities for discovery.

Teach your students about the Learning Cycle. Tell them it is how the brain processes learning.

Answer the Essential Question for Chapter Two

How does neuroscience add to our knowledge of how the Learning Cycle works?

3

The 21st Century Curriculum: Competencies, Concepts and the Common Core

Essential Question

Why is it that the Learning Cycle requires both
competency teaching and the conceptualization of content?

What should all of our students know?
It is simply the wrong question for the 21st
Century. The key question is what
competencies should they have?

Bernice McCarthy, 2012

Competencies, the Foundation and Base of the Learning Cycle

This chapter illustrates how the four Cs: *Communication, Critical Thinking, Collaborative Problem Solving and Creativity* are the foundation of the Learning Cycle and how designing with 4MAT will give you a template for managing the curriculum in your district.

Think of the Learning Cycle and the Competencies as the base of your instructional design.

Competency: the ability to do something well—fluid expertise

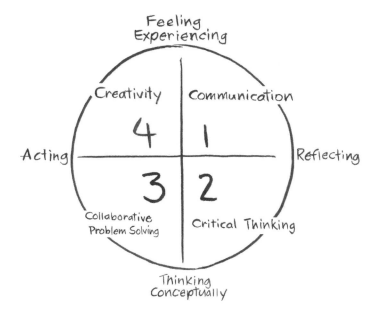

Communication: The Competency Base of Quadrant One

Understanding the "Why?" of Things

> *"Put yourself in conversation with the edge of yourself, no matter how frightening it seems."*
>
> —David Whyte[30]

Quadrant One is set by two parameters, Feeling Experiences and Reflecting on Experiences. Feeling our experiences happens first, then we reflect. We reflect on the feelings that result from our perceptions.

"What just happened?" "Why is this affecting me this way?"

These questions lead us into ourselves, an interpersonal conversation about our feelings. Quadrant One capitalizes on the learner's relationship with the present moment and remembered experiences. After the question, *"What just happened?"* the next question is, *"How am I feeling about what just happened and why?"*

Antonio Damasio[31] speaks of examining our feelings, our perceptions and reactions as a major step in all learning.

First we feel, then we feel the feeling, and sometimes, if we are lionhearted, we examine the "Why?" of the feeling. We apply our core consciousness, a very big and courageous step. Becoming aware of what we are feeling and then examining the why of the feeling is "a revelation of a state of life within us." (Damasio)

This level of personal meaning leads naturally to valuing, the major objective of the first quadrant of The Learning Cycle which is the making of meaning. This meaning-making is the precursor to all learning and an essential form of communication because it is the kind we have with ourselves. When teachers begin with activities that raise this kind of awareness and connect students to past experiences that create meaning for them, they are motivating them to engage more fully. In a sense, they lure them into the learning.

Constructing an experiential activity that captures students and connects them to past meanings causes several things happen:

> The students are pulled into where the learning is going. Not only does it touch their hearts, it pulls them into wider implications of their experiences.
>
> It sets a tone for the importance of the material itself for itself—expert knowledge, the wisdom of the elders.
>
> It presents glimmers of possibilities in students' minds concerning their own becoming.

Skillful communication listens, speaks clearly and authentically, accomplishes meaningful exchanges, influences, cooperates, and assesses reality. These are the attributes to search out when examining the content you must teach regarding this competency.

The Quadrant One Communication Skills Focus

Interior Students' Skills:

Personal awareness of one's own feelings

A sense of freedom and lack of fear to explore these perceptions

A belief in the ability to question them

A fascination with the differences and similarities in the perceptions of others from their own.

Public and External Skills:

To speak authentically of one's feelings

To share surprises and questions about experiences with self and others

To listen well and paraphrase the words of others accurately

To honor the thoughts of others

To disagree with others agreeably

The application of Communication skills is a part of student tasks in all four Learning Cycle quadrants, but the foundation of this competency lies particularly in the ability to communicate through listening and authentic conversation and discussion, and this competency is the base set by the parameters of 4MAT's Quadrant One, Feeling Experience and Reflecting.

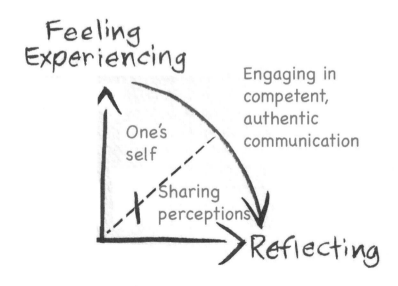

*"The ability to form concepts is bihemispheric,
the right mode forming the visual image,
the left, the semantic relationship.
The combination produces **a total concept**."
(emphasis mine.)*

*D. Frank Benson, Professor of Neurology,
School of Medicine, University of CA*

Critical Thinking: The Competency Base of Quadrant Two

Understanding the "What?" of Things

Quadrant Two is set by two parameters: Thinking Conceptually and Reflecting.

> *"You can know the name of a bird in all the languages of the world, but when you're finished, you'll know absolutely nothing whatever about the bird. So let's look at the bird and see what it's doing, that's what counts. I learned very early the difference between knowing the name of something and knowing something."*

–Richard Feynman,[32] *American physicist*

As the learning process enters the second quadrant of the 4MAT Cycle, the students must capture the essence of the material based on the experiential activity the teacher created in Quadrant One. They must replicate this in some nonverbal way, (metaphors, images, music, sound, etc. images from their own pasts.) Visualizing helps them to achieve clarity about the concept under study, and to know more deeply what the experience means to them. Student images lead to readiness for the words to come, the information and research on the ideas. This combination of visual and semantic is a powerful one and engages both Right- and Left-modes.

In mastering expert knowledge, we ask our students to work in the heart of Critical Thinking, to reason and analyze the "whatness" of ideas and things. The task is to uncover, clarify and understand the "What?" and to do so by sharpening their questioning and critiquing skills. These two steps, the visual imaging and the examining of the expert "word" knowledge through the lecture, the readings and the internet information, combine to create the symbiosis that makes conceptual knowing possible.

Critical thinking clarifies goals, reasons and analyzes, discerns hidden values, examines assumptions, questions evidence, and assesses worthiness. These are the attributes to search out as you examine the content you must teach regarding this competency.

The Quadrant Two Critical Thinking Skills Focus

The Students' Skills:

Ability to understand the expert information conceptually

Ability to grasp the essence, the big idea core of the material

Ability to examine assumptions

Understanding of how the content correlates to other big ideas

The Students' Relationship to the Content:

Belief/skepticism regarding evidence criteria

Agreement/disagreement with expert reasoning

Willingness/unwillingness to revise perspectives

Openness to new values/reinforcement of current values

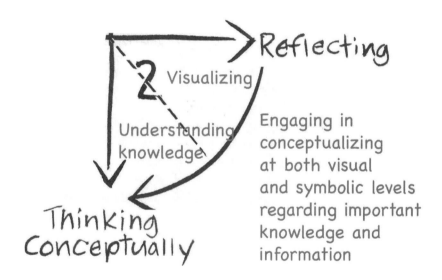

The application of Critical Thinking skills is a part of student tasks in all four Learning Cycle quadrants, but the foundation of this competency lies particularly in the ability to analyze, reason and critique, and this competency is the base set by the parameters of 4MAT's Quadrant Two, Reflecting and Thinking Conceptually.

The vitality of thought is in adventure. Ideas won't keep. Something must be done about them.

Alfred North Whitehead,[33]
English mathematician and philosopher.

Collaborative Problem Solving: The Competency Base of Quadrant Three

Understanding the "How Does This Work?" of Things

Quadrant Three is set by the parameters Thinking Conceptually and Acting.

In Quadrant Three, the 4MAT Learning Cycle enters the doing place, the "How?" place, where the line is crossed from the teacher to the students, where the learners really begin to take over the learning.

This is where students practice learning and discover for themselves if what they are being asked to learn works for them. This is the student figuring out how. How do we solve this problem? How can this be accomplished with high efficiency and doable results? Quadrant Three is where differentiation is the modus operandi. Diverse options become available to the students.

The teacher creates practice activities to assist students in gaining the technical expertise to use the learning in real problem solving. The kinds of practice must differentiate enough to reach all the students: the traditional ways of pen and pencil, workbooks, and printed materials, with lots of online materials, both words and images, different student groupings, all designed to give as many opportunities as particular students need to achieve the technical skills to master the learning. It includes multiple practices all the way from simple to complex, various student groupings, all with the same learning goals but offering different pathways. The students' abilities are first practiced in the Left-Mode section of Quadrant Three, followed by collaborative problem solving with real life problems in the Right Mode, Extend, section of this quadrant.

> *"Collaboration is a coordinated, synchronous activity that is the result of a continued attempt to construct and maintain a shared conception of a problem.*
>
> *...Collaborative problem solving does not just happen because individuals are co-present; individuals must make a conscious, continued effort to coordinate their language and activity with respect to shared knowledge. The most important resource for collaboration is talk.*
>
> *Collaborators use the overall turn-taking structure of talk allowing participants to produce shared knowledge, to recognize divergent understandings, and to rectify problems that impeded joint agreement."*
>
> *–Jeremy Roschellel and Stephanie D. Teasley,*[34] *1995, Collaborative Problem Solving*

This is the part of teaching that lifts the heart of the teacher, listening and observing as the students engage one another. Commitment to the success of the group, coordinating activities, recognizing divergent understandings, and producing shared knowledge are the attributes to search for in the content you must teach regarding this competency.

The Quadrant Three Collaborative Problem Solving Focus

Students' Practice Skills

Understanding the expert information conceptually

Exploring evidence criteria

Determining patterns

Questioning assumptions

Improving ability to manipulate data

Students' Collaborative Work
(Learning is fundamentally a social activity.)

To enter into the logic of problem solving

To construct shared knowledge

To recognize divergent understandings, and

To rectify problems that impede joint agreement

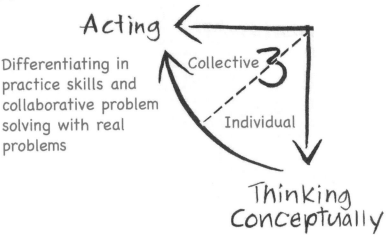

The application of Collaborative Problem Solving skills is a part of student tasks in all four Learning Cycle quadrants, but the foundation of this competency lies in the ability to experiment, tinker and gain expertise in problem solving together and this is the base set by the parameters of 4MAT's Quadrant Three, Thinking Conceptually and Acting.

Creativity needs to be as important as literacy in our schools.

Sir Ken Robinson,[35]
Education and creativity expert

Creativity: The Competency Base of Quadrant Four

Understanding the "If?" of Things

Quadrant Four is set by two parameters: Acting and Feeling Experience.

The creativity competency lies in the ability of students to adapt the learning into their own lives, into the time and place where they live. This adaptation is naturally unique to them, so in some sense it is always original. The teacher's task is to create appealing options that lead to interesting performances that integrate the learning, to monitor and support for rigor and to make sure the students follow through. The ultimate integration would be student sharing of their unique adaptations in ways that would benefit the larger community.

In the Left Mode of Quadrant Four, students refine and polish their learning performances: their readings, writings, dramas, science experiments conclusion reports, research, interviews, journal articles, all with rigorous rubrics, preferably created together by teacher and students.

The Quadrant Four Creativity Focus

Student Polishing and Refining Skills

Applying the rubric to their work

Being critiqued by teacher and peers

Being open to suggestions for improvement

Persevering for back up re-drawing or revising

Checking for possible unintended outcomes

Student Performance

Originality as clearly described in (joint) rubric

Impact on listeners, audience

Larger audience engagements

Better questions, better formulating analyses

Integration of the learning into student's real life and the greater community

Rubric polishing

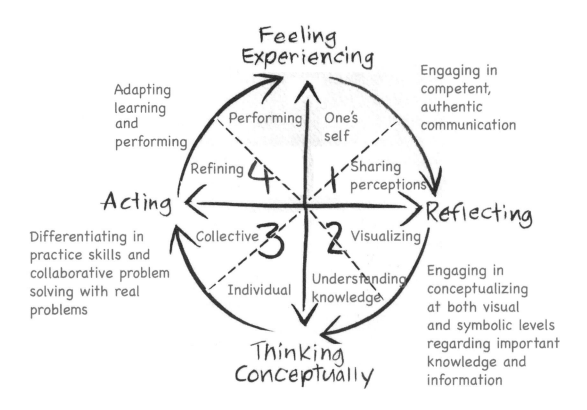

Feeling
Experiencing

Engaging in
competent,
authentic
communication

Adapting
learning
and
performing

Performing   One's
self

Refining 4   Sharing
perceptions

Acting   Reflecting

Differentiating in
practice skills and
collaborative problem
solving with real
problems

Collective 3   2 Visualizing

Individual   Understanding
knowledge

Engaging in
conceptualizing
at both visual
and symbolic levels
regarding important
knowledge and
information

Thinking
Conceptually

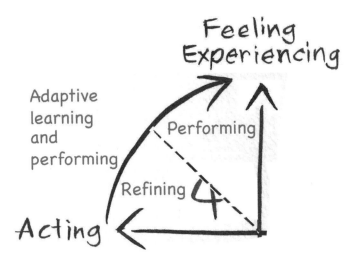

Feeling
Experiencing

Adaptive
learning
and
performing

Performing

Refining

4

Acting

The application of Creativity skills is a part of student tasks in all four Learning Cycle quadrants, but the foundation of this competency lies within the ability to integrate learning by adapting it which is the competency base set by the parameters of 4MAT's Quadrant Four, Acting and Feeling Experience.

Notice the difference in learning tasks as instruction moves around the Cycle–from Why? to What? to How? and to If? The teacher's roles change as well; from Motivator, to Instructor, to Coach/Facilitator, to Critic and Cheerleader.

I believe the single most important feature of the Cycle is its emphasis on the primacy of direct experience.

David Hunt,[36] 1987

Concepts: The Core of the Instructional Design

The 4MAT Learning Cycle is the process you need to insure that your teaching stays focused on the crucial structures of your content, the significant concepts with the 4Cs competencies base. You simply cannot create a 4MAT instructional design if you do not conceptualize. It is the process you need.

Think of competencies as nouns, your intended learning results, and the primary focus of your teaching. If your graduating students excel at: communicating both within themselves and with others authentically, are critical thinkers, have the ability to solve problems both individually and collectively and engage in original innovative work, you have done a fine job of educating them. Focus on these competencies as you design, teach and assess your instruction.

If competencies are the nouns, then conceptualizing is the verb. It is the process you will use to do this. Conceptualizing is the skill of the master teacher. 4MAT is the template for putting this process into effect. You must begin by answering the question: What are you teaching? The answer to the "What" question is the key, both at the highest levels of graduate school and at primary school literacy level and this is true in all content areas. You must approach the what question conceptually.

Concept: a key idea for a body of content, the inherent essence that connects to other key ideas and also will form connections to particular students. It is like a path through a overgrown forest.

Content: the expert knowledge, information and details to be mastered as topical to the Concept. When learning material is approached conceptually instead of topically, it is like smoothing a path through a forest or even a jungle. If you choose the concept well, it forms connections in student hearts and minds based on the lives they are living. Then the details make sense and are learned in the learning, not separated to be memorized. Clearly, the teacher must know not only the content but also know his or her students as well. When you design instruction with the Learning Cycle as your template, your teaching is experiential, that is, it begins with an experience of the Concept, a happening, not a telling of it. The experience must intrigue your learners, so you must know their world and capture it in your concept choice.

Essence: substance, central theme, heart of the matter, nub, kernel, marrow, meat, crux, thrust, drift, sense, meaning, significance, import, nitty-gritty, quintessence, soul, spirit, nature, core, nucleus, substance, principle, fundamental quality, warp and woof

Sadly it appears that our textbooks continue to be distorted by a commercial textbook market that requires that they cover the entire range of facts about biology, thereby sacrificing the opportunity to treat the central **concepts** *in enough depth to give our students a chance to truly understand them.*
(emphasis mine)

American Association for the Advancement of Science, June, 2000

All of the above work for me. A concept is a choice the teacher makes based on several factors: level of knowledge of the content, knowledge of the particular students, and her or his ability to conceptualize. John Goodlad[37] spoke of concept teaching back in 1982 in his best selling book, *A Place Called School*. He gathered research from 27,000 students, teachers and parents, and maintained that *"the core of education should be a set of concepts, principles, and skills, and ways of knowing, not topics."* The reason for the lack of conceptual teaching in schools, he went on to explain, was that *"unfortunately, most teachers are not deeply immersed in the concepts that provide structure to the fields of knowledge."* He suggested that *"we need to engage in analysis of the subject fields and clarify what the concepts are."*

The concepts you choose and the experiences you create based on them, will lead your students directly to the content with higher motivation.

Concept Characteristics

They are generalizable, they have universal application leading to larger purposes than the content itself, enhancing broader meaning and valuing.

They cross disciplines and connect to other significant concepts.

James Rutherford's Project 2061 Research on Important Science Concepts

James Rutherford's[38] **Project 2061** is an example of conceptualizing content in science. Effort was focused on deciding which concepts form the structural questions and themes that underlie science. *"We will get away from fighting over a finite piece of time in a class to examine underlying themes connected to some richer fabric."*

In *Science for All Americans,* his group listed five themes as the structural basis and most significant science concepts. The five were: system, change, constancy, model and scale.

Whether or not you agree with these five choices (and the Common Core writers are reexamining science concepts as of this writing), the common sense reason is simply that the plethora of content and the amount of information teachers are attempting to manage make it imperative to teach from core themes and structures. Rutherford reported the 300 to 350 pages of science per year contained 2,400 to 3,000 symbols. The average high school textbook introduces 7 to 10 new concepts per page. In a school year of 180 days that would mean covering 20 concepts per class or 1 every 2 minutes. Small wonder teachers are frustrated, students bored silly and scholars write negative reviews.

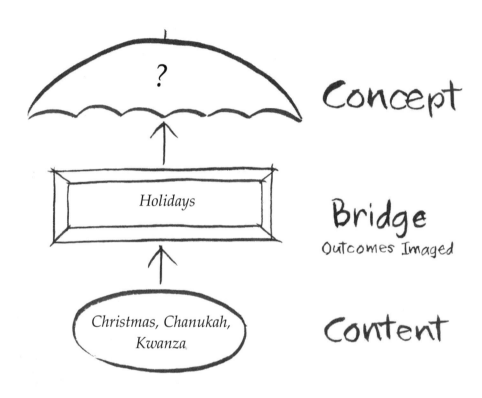

A Concept/Content Umbrella

Albert Einstein understood the problem well.

"But in physics I soon learned to scent out the paths that led to the depths, and to disregard everything else, all the many things that clutter up the mind and divert it from the essential. The hitch in this was of course, the fact that one had to cram all of this stuff into one's mind for the examination, whether one like it or not."

21st century curriculum must focus on competencies and concepts, the connections and relationships among ideas and disciplines, forsaking the ubiquitous and often separate and isolated content approaches of the 20th century, "inch deep" memorizing.

How Do Teachers Conceptualize Their Content?

Simple, they umbrella it.

Try it yourself. Imagine that the content of your unit is the three mid-winter events of Christmas, Chanukah, Kwanza, and you are teaching primary students. I have put the content in the oval at the bottom of the umbrella graphic on the facing page.

Now go up to the middle frame **(Bridge)** and think of a big idea for those three events? Elevate the content to a higher, more generalizable level.

How about *Holidays?* That could be a big idea that primary children would understand. I call that second step, the **Bridge,** because it is a bridge from the content to the concept, a stepping stone as it were. Okay, put Holidays in that middle frame.

Now go up one more step to the top umbrella to find the best most encompassing and meaningful big idea that Holidays represents. Where might Holidays lead you?

It would have to be significant learning in the minds of young children. It should be something they have experienced but perhaps never thought about that way. It should be something you could replicate in the classroom experientially to begin the unit.

Whatever you choose, that would be your unit **Concept**.

Of course several fine teachers could each come up with a different and equally well suited choice. Write yours in the overarching concept umbrella at the top of the graphic. After you choose yours, turn the page and see the one I chose.

Remember mine may not be better than yours, they could both be great examples of how to teach these three holidays. Whatever you choose for that top umbrella will be the core of your opening activity as you begin to teach the content. This will be explained in detail in the next chapter.

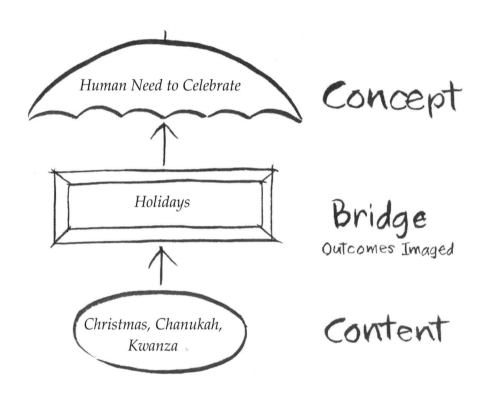

A Concept/Content Umbrella

I chose for my top umbrella *"The Human Need to Celebrate."* That was my concept.

Now what would you rather teach, three holidays in and of themselves or a concept about the human need to celebrate? By capturing this big idea, students will relate to these three different cultural events as examples of humans celebrating, which has meaning for them and which leads them to a larger purpose than the content itself.

Your choice needs to be significant and therefore valuable and meaningful to your students. What if you decided the diversity of these mid-winter cultural celebrations would be a big idea for your group? What could the Bridge be, what would the Concept be?

The answer is it depends. It depends on you and your students, your knowledge of the cultural backgrounds of all three celebrations and how you want to focus your instructional design.

Maddening isn't it, with no one right answer. That's what makes us professionals, not technicians–our judgements about how the content we must teach fits with our students and the big ideas that connect them. **Competencies, Concepts and Content,** *instead of just Content.*

Content: The Stuff We Teach – Information, knowledge and skills with the standards and benchmarks and details necessary to support what you are required to teach.

More Practice on Conceptualizing Content

A well chosen concept that captures the essence of the content will give you the basis for the experience you create at the beginning of the lesson or unit. If it resonates with your students and their lives, they will connect to the value of the learning.

Examine these two examples.

> If you are to teach Columbus and Magellan to 8 to 10 year-olds, you might begin with Exploration. They know all about exploration and they love it. Come up with an exploring activity that can happen right in the classroom or the school proper and let them experience exploring. Let them note the perseverance and courage it takes to explore when you really don't know how things will turn out.

Your evaluation of the content essence

The Content

The concept is the power that a particular image has standing for or conveying a certain meaning or intellectual value. The Concept is something which the image does; some meaning which it conveys. The concept arises from realizing the full meaning of the perception. The image is more than an abstraction, it is an extraction, an intuitive registering in the brain. The concept becomes an enriching of the meaning of the perception.

John Dewey,[39] 1965

Or teach Scientific Inquiry to middle schoolers by starting with Wonder, they get that. You just have to come up with an opening activity that will excite wonder in them.

A successful, engaging experience that is shared and discussed flows right into the Right-mode image of the concept-based experience. This is the **Bridge**, the connection of the content to the concept. It is a non-verbal representational image: visual (drawn, created or found) or auditory (musical piece, other type of sound) or kinesthetic (acted out) relationship between the two. In a senior unit on *"Man's Inhumanity to Man,"* one of my students chose as his image, the sound of prison doors slamming shut.

In the Dewey quote on the preceeding page, note especially he calls the image creating an extraction (think tooth), a pulling out of the learner's connection to the concept **before the lecture begins.** The learners become in tuned with the expert knowledge.

Images of all three types, visual, auditory and kinesthetic, are important and powerful strategies. They help students formulate their own personal notions of the concept.

Images give us relationships, evoke memories, and past stories. Encourage and honor these in your students.

Take the science example. What image might help a student understand the relationship between scientific inquiry and wonder? Could it be *progress* or at least the *road to progress?* If the students image a road to progress as the result of a scientist's wondering, have you increased the retention odds for leveraging student impact?

Here's another example, this one from mathematics, Algebra One, teaching polynomials. The concept the authors of our *4MAT Algebra Course* chose is "Patterns," and the bridge is "Simplification." The content is polynomials. Polynomials are different powers of the same variable. Patterns lend themselves to understanding the meaning and purpose of them. In this unit the teacher chose as the Quadrant One, Right Mode, Connect, a Discovery Zone activity. The students find it on the Golden Ration Website, http://goldennumber.net/body.htm. Check it out, it is great fun as the students report.

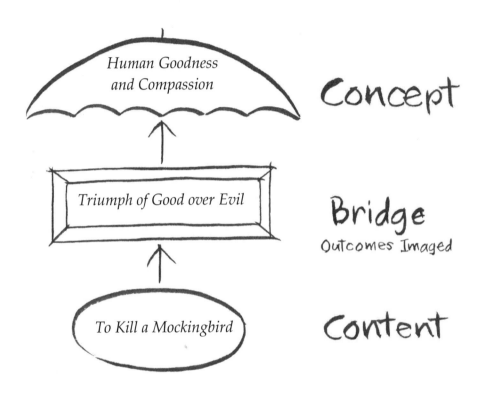

Concept

Bridge
Outcomes Imaged

Content

A Concept/Content Umbrella

In literature we wrote a course for the novel, *To Kill a Mockingbird* by Harper Lee. The novel relates tragedy and injustice, but it also illustrates courage, and awareness of the better side of human beings. What concept might you choose to teach this book?

concept	I choose *Human Goodness and Compassion*. The author, Harper Lee, sets up characters in each chapter, that regardless of how strange or unfriendly or annoying they are, perform both small and large acts of compassion.
bridge (outcomes imaged)	For the bridge, I looked at the results of the actions in the book and found redemption and courage. I chose the triumph of good over evil. That is the learning result I wanted students to get from reading the book, that they would experience, at least hypothetically, such triumph and perhaps make them more amenable to believe such things are so.
content	The content was *To Kill a Mockingbird* by Harper Lee.

The **Bridge** is the link from the content to the concept. The Bridge imprints the importance of the chosen concept clearly in your students' minds by having them create a related image. But the Bridge is even more important than that!

It is the image of your hoped-for outcome, your learning results, your raison d'être for teaching the unit.

Think about the relationship I wanted students to discover as they read this book. My planned outcome was for them to discover that in the world of human suffering, compassion triumphs often, if not always.

Or the example of the science unit in inquiry, that wonder and curiosity results in progress that could benefit all. Think of the mental processing required here. The image has a double payoff.

First, you can easily and quickly find out if a student understands the relationship of the experience you created in Quadrant One. You see the image, you hear the sounds, you watch the movement, and you know whether or not the student understands the concept.

Second, the student comes to understand better what s/he means in thinking about and creating the image. Their choices reflect who they are and their past experiences. These images need to be brought into the discussions, be referred to and enlarged in the lecture.

The Bridge is the image of the relationship between the learning and the students own lives and most importantly, the outcome of the lesson.

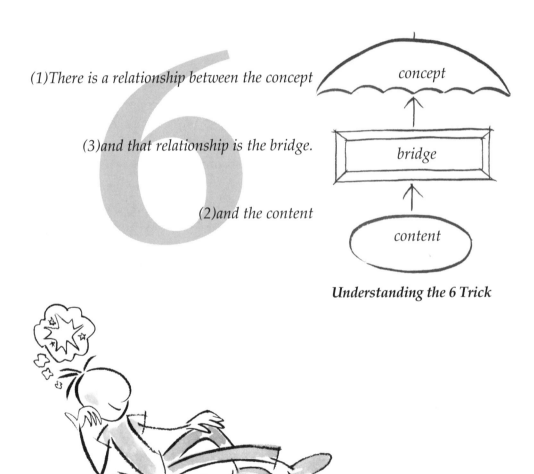

(1)There is a relationship between the concept

(3)and that relationship is the bridge.

(2)and the content

concept

bridge

content

Understanding the 6 Trick

The 6 Trick and the Umbrella

This is a very cool strategy. It is not mine. It was discovered by a fine teacher who worked with me for a while then taught the Learning Cycle in an education graduate class.

The simplest way to choose your best concept and most elegant bridge is to use the Umbrella 6 Trick to make your concept and bridge choices. This graphic device tells you if your choices are conceptually cohesive. If they are, they will work in your total plan.

Here are the questions to ask yourself.

Does your concept contain a key part of the content?

Will your concept be interesting, motivating and maybe even exciting to your learners?

Is the Bridge the one you want to establish a relationship between the concept and the content?

Run this sentence through your mind to see how it works for you. Try it with something you have taught.

*There is a relationship between the **Concept** (the Big Idea),* _____

(your concept here)

*and the material to be taught, the **Content**,* _____

(your content here)

*and that relationship is the **Bridge**, (the outcome imaged).* _____

(your bridge here)

Picture yourself swooping a big six from the top of the umbrella, down around the content and curving up to point to and end with the Bridge.

It makes all kinds of sense and it will show you if you have an elegant plan.

You begin the Learning Cycle experientially epitomizing your concept and you return to it with your students integrating the learning into their own lives.

The following chapter explains how to put this all together–how to design your teaching with the four competencies as the Cycle foundation, conceptualizing content and using the processes of both hemispheres.

Sounds like deer in the headlights doesn't it? Well it is at first. But once you master it, your planning will be more motivating, important knowledge will be more deeply examined, you will be creating more differentiated skill practices, and you and your students will be rewarded with more successful learning results.

But first you have to see how to use the benefits of the Common Core Standards as your guidelines.

The Content You Teach Using Examples from the Common Core Standards

Start by separating your content into the 4MAT Quadrants in this way:

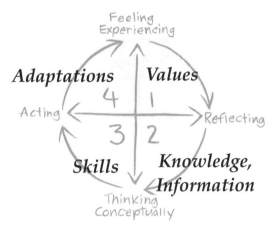

The bottom half of the 4MAT Learning Cycle is where you find your content and your skills. That is the knowledge they need to know; those are the skills they need to use it.

Scaffolding is differentiated learning and a necessary tool in the hands of teachers. Instructional scaffolding is a learning process designed to promote a deeper learning. Scaffolding is the support given during the learning process which is tailored to the needs of the student with the intention of helping the student achieve his/her learning goals .

Instructional scaffolding is the provision of sufficient support to promote learning when concepts and skills are being first introduced to students, as with resources, guides, coaching.

Robert Keith Sawyer,[41] *2006*

That is the beauty of the Common Core Standards. They delineate the best and most rigorous descriptions of what ALL students need to know to live well in the 21st Century. Understand that the common core standards are not a curriculum. They are a clear set of shared goals and expectations for what knowledge and skills are required in this age. And as such, they are a guide *but only for the bottom half of the Learning Cycle.* It is your job as a professional educator to bring this knowledge and these skills to your learners with your instructional designs, motivating them to value the learning and guiding them to adapt and integrate it into their lives, completing the whole Cycle. You are the curriculum decider, with your district guides, your professional content knowledge and your caring interest in your learners guided by the rigor of the Common Core.

Examine these examples from the Common Core[40] and see which of the four categories of the 4MAT Cycle you think they cover: students **valuing** the learning, students understanding the **knowledge and information**, students having the **skills** to do these things and students **adapting** these learnings into their lives. Which of these four?

Common Core Examples

Literacy Examples

With prompting and support, read prose and poetry (informational texts) of appropriate complexity for Grade 1.

By the end of grade 11, read and comprehend literature (informational texts, history/social studies texts, science/technical texts) with scaffolding as needed at the high of the required range.

Language Progressive Skills Examples

Ensure subject-verb and pronoun-antecedent agreement.

Choose words and phrases to convey ideas precisely.

Mathematics Examples

Grade 2: Measurement and Data

Grade 8: Statistics and probability

High School: Using Models

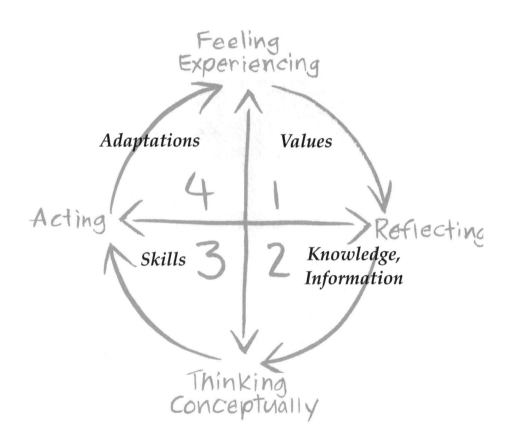

The Standards for Mathematical Practice describe varieties of expertise that mathematics educators at all levels should seek to develop. Here are three of them.

1. Make sense of problems and persevere in solving them.

2. Reason abstractly and quantitatively—creating representations of problems.

3. Construct viable arguments and critique the reasoning of others.

Clearly these seem to be all primarily skills, but are they?

These descriptions illustrate the current shift taking place in education from content to competencies. The teacher's task is how to focus on what students can do with what they are learning. But the doing must be from their own valuing and must lead them to their own integration of what they are learning. Take the Common Core Standards, or whatever curriculum requirements you have to teach in your content area. Get together with your team of teachers. (And heaven forbid, if you do not have one, talk to your principal. Everyone should be in a team.) Get together and make copies of the curriculum and the standards you have to teach and cluster them.

On large paper use a stream of consciousness rather than any analysis technique at first. After brainstorming, look for similar patterns of values, content big ideas and information, skills, and possible adaptations. These are the key elements of the 4MAT Learning Cycle.

Create lists of all four. What could go where? Where does grammar go? How about statistical data, how about constitutional law, how about a fine piece of literature, Mary Oliver's poetry? Rap, Harry Potter, and so on.

Could some be in more than one place, what will fit your students, this year, in the place where you live? What does your curriculum stress, what are the patterns you see? What do you fellow teachers think about these things. Can you work together on which connections would be the most important for your students?

Create your lists and begin the task of applying teaching strategies in all four quadrants. Can your choices for reading assignments be enhanced by focusing on stories where the main characters tackle a difficult problem as you keep Collaborative Problem Solving in mind?

Can you let your concern, for example, with a seeming lack of Creativity in your students move you to motivate them to write about an issue of fairness involving real people in your community for publication in a local blog or paper?

Or have them research a Values issue, a busy corner near the school and count the number of times cars do not come to a complete stop and report back. Then what could they do with that information? What kind of communication could you build into the next step? What skills? Where could it take them?

The more you think about the four competencies, and how to cluster your "must teach" content, the easier it will be to for you to create exciting feeling, reflecting, thinking and doing tasks.

Answer the Essential Question for Chapter Three

Why is it that the Learning Cycle requires both competency teaching and the conceptualization of content?

4

Teaching the 21ˢᵗ Century Learner with the 4MAT Learning Cycle

Essential Question

How can teachers master the flow around the Cycle?

I wouldn't give a fig for simplicity
this side of complexity
but I would give my life for simplicity
on the other side of complexity.

Oliver Wendell Holmes[42]

Teaching the 21st Century Learner Around the Cycle

"The journey from brain to mind is through experience."

–James Zull

...exactly where the Learning Cycle begins. It is elegantly simple. We all do it naturally, but sadly, not often enough in school.

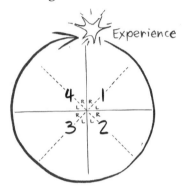

For example, think about learning a new word, one you have never heard before. You're a high school sophomore. *"Anachronistic."*

"Why do I need to know that word? It doesn't sound like a word I would ever use?"

Your chosen study group leader snaps back, "Because you signed up for our study group to go over the SAT practice words, that's why."

"OK, you're right, I don't know it. What does it mean?"

"It means old fashioned, conspicuously old fashioned."

"Really, I could never have guessed that."

"You wouldn't have to guess if you knew its roots."

You are curious, it interests you enough that you want to know where a word that sounds a bit like a movie you saw about spiders came from. So you go to the Dictionary to find the root. Dictionary: Anachronistic, old fashioned, ana- 'backward' + khronos 'time.' to go back in time.

"Yea, that makes sense," you say, "backwards in time."

You decide to use "anachronistic" on your teenage sister the next time she puts something new on and asks you how you like it.

"That outfit is a bit anachronistic, isn't it?"

All knowing starts with identification,
with experience. We are in it to begin with.

Mary Catherine Bateson,[43] *1994*

Your mother's jaw drops a bit and in the end you all have a good laugh. Six months later you take the SAT verbal test and guess what. There it is: anachronistic. Bet you'll never forget that word.

You and your group also discovered more than just the meaning of anachronistic. You zeroed in on other words that have khronos for roots, using both c and k. You found quite a few:

chronicle, chronometer, Chronos the Greek god of time, crone, chronic, chronology.

Now that word and its root belongs to you, our imaginary sophomore. You have gone around the entire learning cycle, the complete learning act, from **Why** do I want to know this? to **What** is it? to **How** can I use it? to **If** I learn it what will I be better able to do? Simple and elegant.

What competencies were in play in when you went through this imaginary simple learning example? **Communication,** of course. But think more deeply about what kind of communication.

Obviously the easy answer is vocabulary. But there is more. You went into the "What" of the word more deeply and you analyzed the heart of the meaning. Then with a morbid sense of humor you hassled your sister with it. Then you got one point higher on your verbal SAT. You mastered your learning in a situation in your own life.

I am suggesting throughout this book that traveling the Cycle is always a complete learning act.

I further maintain that our educational system has left out Quadrants One and Four, the **Why?** and **If?** questions, to serious disadvantage, and failed to see the adaptive nature of both of these ways of being and their function in a complete Learning Cycle. The **Why?** and **If?** questions require us to adapt to rapid change with meaning making leading the way. The technical skills of the Millennials are expanding rapidly as they come to understand global unity and interactions. They are mastering both technical and adaptive skills, the complete Cycle.

The Millennials have not left out the **Why?** and the **If?** That is where they live.

1. They believe in networking.   **Why** are we here? To work together.

2. They have access to huge amount of expert knowledge   **What?**

3. They are committed to Stewardship*   **How?**

4. They are certain they can create and implement innovative solutions   **If?**

Stewardship: a view on how we respect the world and the surrounding environment: economic, health, property, information, religion—aligned collaborative problem solving and the concept of sustainability.

They are excellent at finding the *What?* and major concerned with the *How?*—how to make a difference—but they live in the *Why?* and the *If?* They diagnose the why of things in context as it shifts and emerges and they rate high in the imaginative *If?* along with the technology to create it.

My prediction, they most certainly will.

The Learning Cycle Teaching Template

Creating Quadrant One: Experiencing and Communicating Core Concepts

Experiences activate neurons which create new connections. Think of learning to play the trumpet. After only a few lessons you are playing it, albeit ineptly. Your teacher helps you place your fingers in a more suitable position, comes around behind you and helps you hold the instrument at the angle that best releases your breath, and tells you that you are doing great. You begin by experiencing the trumpet.

The art teacher has you play with color. The coach watches you run on your first track practice. The art and music teacher and the coach begin where students are. They pay attention to individual potential. They focus on what is present in the student including things not easily seen: motivation, a sense of wholeness about the work, a quality of perseverance. They try to capture the uniqueness of each child.

"Let me see you handle this ball."

"Look at these works of art other students are working on. Tell me what you like and why."

"Try to make a note with this trumpet, any note."

If whatever is new to experience is more likely to be present in the right hemisphere, this suggests a temporal hierarchy of attention, with our awareness of any object of experience beginning in the right hemisphere, which grounds experience, before it gets to be further processed in the left hemisphere.

Iain McGilchrist,[44] 2009

How is it that art, music teachers and coaches always begin with their students' experiences and the majority of teachers do not? Somehow they know experience activates the brain's natural propensity for connections. Students' past experiences influence who they are and teachers need to draw forth that remembering.

The introduction of all new learning needs to begin with an experience that is felt, is attended to and creates meaning.

Another Look at the Quadrant One Parameters

The parameters that form Quadrant One are *"feeling experiences"* and *"reflecting on those experiences."* These dimensions of feeling and reflecting require that teachers choose strategies that affect students' hearts not just their heads. The opening activity must engage the students' emotions, arousing curiosity as to the value of what they are about to learn. If they can't see any value, the task becomes mindless to them. When this happens, some dutifully do what the teacher wants, others just check out.

Teaching Strategies for Quadrant One

Lesson on Fractions

Begin with an experience that contains the key concept you have chosen for the content. Do not begin with direct content. If you were teaching fractions for example, you would not begin by showing them how to do fractions. Save the specific explanations and skills for later after students become engaged in "fractionness. You must first bring them to the place where they are keen to know. Create an experiential activity that encompasses the overarching concept of "fractionness," an experience that contains the core meaning of it.

What is the core meaning of fractions? Now there's a question. What is it? Don't be put off if you have to think about this for a minute or two because in order to do this task you have to conceptualize, and conceptualizing takes a fairly high level of thinking. Examine some possibilities that come to mind that you might use to conceptualize *"fractionness"* for young children.

How about whole to part? Could that be a significant concept for fractions? Here is a possible activity. Give each child six small pieces of paper, about 3 inches by 3 inches, have the students draw one of their arms, and then the other on a separate piece of paper. Next they draw one leg, then the other, then a head, then a body. Now the

Understanding can be symbolized through words,
but understanding itself requires language no more
than a bird requires a cage. Understanding comes
only through experience. And for experience, there
has never been, and never will be, a substitute.

Ken Carey,[45] *1991*

The effective teacher builds on exploration
of what students already know and believe,
and the sense they have made of it.

David Kolb,[46] *1982*

students have six drawings on six pieces of paper. Give them a larger seventh paper and have them cut out their six parts and mount them on the larger paper making themselves whole again.

Or how about the ability to divide things so everyone is treated fairly? Would that work with your students? Bring cookies with not enough for everyone. The children must figure out what to do.

Or how about parts fitting together from cut up pictures?

Follow up these activities with small groups of students creating lists of characteristics of whole things and parts of things.The students will get the Big Idea with any one of these strategies. They will understand the key concept of *"fractionness"* before you teach them how to do the math. This is where you want them to be when you begin the number manipulations, understanding why fractions are important, that all whole things are made up of parts. The opening experience you devise must contain one of the major concepts of the content that will connect to your learners as opposed to manipulating numbers without any clarity of what the manipulation is for.

Lesson on *Brahms Requiem* by Frank Abrahams, Rider University

Students make a playlist of songs for one who has experienced a loss. Students prepare a playlist of songs from their own library of tunes that one might give to a person who has experienced a loss. They burn a CD to share with the class and for the teacher. In journals, or on a class blog, or in a class discussion, they describe the criteria (rubric) they used to select each example.

This leads students to a discussion on the issue of relevancy. After sharing selections from the various playlists, students wrestle with the question of relevancy. In class, or in their journals or class blog, they discuss how music of the past can be relevant in today's culture and in their own particular world and lives . Does music mirror culture? Can we understand the past by listening to and studying the music of a particular period in time?

Teaching Strategy: Have the students step into a painting and remain there for thirty minutes recording their observations in their journals.

> *Use in History:* They are on board with George Washington crossing the Delaware. Many such paintings of this scene can be found on Google, pick one that will suit your students. Maybe they could even try to find out who else was in the boat.

Teaching Strategy: Journal writing assuming another persona.

Use in Literature: Assign a three-page journal entry in prose or poetry that could have been written by Emily Dickinson right after a first snow fall.

Teaching Strategy: Simulation–create an interesting situation where students must play the parts

Use in Government Studies: Intro to the Constitutional Convention. Student groups simulate elders in two villages in the 16th century deciding to merge into one governing body to facilitate the growth of their economies. One has a small population, the other twice as large. How do they decide on the number of voting representatives that should come from each village for the governing board they are creating? The larger village says it should be done by population, the smaller says not fair. Students must work it out and report on their solution.

Or you could give them another task. One of the villages has outlawed slavery, the other's economic health depends on slaves. How do they solve this one? What compromise?

Teaching Strategy: Brainstorm a world without shapes

Use in Geometry One: Intro to a Geometry unit
Objective: To engage students in the awareness that geometry is all around us.
Activity: Working in cooperative learning groups, students are challenged first to brainstorm examples of all things in our natural world that are not basically shaped in the form of cylinders or circles, cubes or squares, pyramids or triangles, or formed from either curved or straight connecting lines. Second they are challenged to brainstorm a list of all things made by man that do not have the same criteria.

Students post lists based on their collective brainstorming. The class as a whole decides if all items meet the set criteria. Their lists will be all liquids or gases; they will discover that all solids have a basic geometric shape or combination of shapes.

I take pictures of real world problems.
Then make the questions irresistible so they
have to find the answer.

Dan Meyer,[47] Math Teacher, 2010

Creating Quadrant Two: Critical Thinking with Big Ideas

The brain goes for the big ideas, then fills in the details. We teach backwards to the brain's way of learning. We teach the details and then test students to death, and along the way they hopefully get the big ideas. This is particularly true in math. The details are worthless without the big ideas they serve.

Try these three math terms. What are the big ideas? You were taught them. Do you remember? How often do you use these skills today? Try playing with the big ideas for Absolute Value, Algorithm and the Frequency Distribution Table.

Absolute Value: The distance a number is from zero.

Make each student a number and line them up in order going two directions away from the student who is the zero. Ask them how important it might be to know how far one is from zero. See what they come up with. (It will be credit cards every time.)

Algorithm: a step-by-step way to find an answer to something. Have them give you non-math examples of how a step-by-step procedure would help them do something they wanted to do. Create this discussion before you teach them to add, subtract, multiply and divide.

Frequency Distribution Table: What might you devise for your students to do that they are curious about where a frequency distribution would come in handy? Ask them. You'll be amazed at what they want to know. Then have them create one.

Three Big Ideas

The absolute value is closely related to the notions of magnitude, distance and norm in various mathematical and physical contexts. Pick the big idea that suits you and you students to introduce absolute value.

We use algorithms every day. A recipe for baking a cake is an algorithm. Most programs consist of algorithms. Inventing elegant algorithms that are simple and require the fewest steps possible is one of the principal challenges in programming, as well as any formula or set of steps for solving a particular problem. The algorithm's set of rules must be unambiguous and have a clear stopping point. Which concept might you choose to introduce algorithms to your students?

Schools organize the work of students around discrete bits without paying attention to what is going on in other bits...and the bits don't connect in any meaningful way.

Richard Elmore,[48] *2004*

A frequency distribution shows us a summarized way to group and organize data: results of an election, team stats, sales of a product within a certain period, student loan amounts owed by graduates. Which of these would you choose to get your students engaged? If they get the big idea, they will do well when tested on the details. If your opening conceptual activity inspires curiosity to find answers to some question about a big idea, they will figure out the details as they go. They will learn it in the doing of it. For an excellent example of this, check out Dan Meyer's presentation on TED.

Another Look at the Quadrant Two Parameters

The parameters that form Quadrant Two are *"reflecting on our experiences"* and *"thinking conceptually."* This requires examining expert knowledge. These parameters require that content ideas and knowledge be taught through the overarching concept you have selected as key to your content.

Teaching Strategies for Quadrant Two

> *Surprisingly our biology textbooks are filled with unnecessary detail, they provide only fragmentary treatment of fundamentally important concepts.*
>
> *—George Nelson,[49] 1991*

Your task is to help students see the information in the context of some larger concept, and to be skeptical and critically adept. Know your material well and explain to your students how you learned it. Begin with a fascinating "Why?" question to focus them on real life issues as you go through the lecture. Limit teacher-directed explanations of information to small segments, somewhere around twenty minutes. Teach only what can be comfortably grasped in the allotted time–two or three important points with illustrated examples. However, if you intersperse time for small group work into the lecture for student critiquing of the main ideas, you could extend the "telling" segment a bit longer. I highly recommend small group brief task discussions during your lectures. Also trust your students to learn some of the key materials on their own and be clear about the tasks you require.

Embed the Learning Cycle into teacher-directed lectures: from including the Quadrant One *"Why?"* to having students use graphic organizer notes. Make the information you deliver provocative. Have them compare and contrast, analyze and synthesize while listening. Teach them to use graphic organizers for note-taking in addition to their regular vizualization practices for recording key information. Use

Sadly, our biology books continue to be distorted by a textbook market that requires they cover the entire range of facts about biology, sacrificing the opportunity to treat the central concepts in enough depth to give students a chance to truly understand them.

Bruce Alberts,[50] 1991

People build their mental representations to impose order and coherence on experience and information.

Jean Piaget,[51] 1951

case studies in your lectures with the students figuring out how these cases were actually resolved as you progress through the lecture. Above all teach them to question, to check facts, to dig into data. Give them practice with bad data. Tell them you have inserted some and challenge them to find it.

Teaching Strategies for Quadrant Two

Teaching Strategy: Comparing past dilemmas with current ones

Use in History: Explain and use direct quotes from the argument between Jefferson and Adams concerning the ability or inability of "the people" to make serious decisions regarding the governance of their new country. Follow with a discussion of Adam's fear and Jefferson's beliefs that the people could be trusted to think well. Discuss whether this is still an issue today. Have the students list positives and negatives on both sides.

Teaching Strategy: Solving a problem while listening to the lecture

Use in Biology: Using Balance as the core concept, teach how cells regulate a balance between their internal and external environments by having the students reason through the task by simulating a cell carrying out a specific task. Build into lectures the beginning of the skills they will need to learn. Here is another example from the work of Charles Darwin. Ask students to focus on the following questions at the beginning of the lecture as they watch the film of his work in the Galapagos. Why was Darwin concerned with the differences in finches related to adaptation? What is your hunch? What process in the man delivered that insight? Was it innate? Or given the same background as his, could anyone have come up with that insight? *(Many of our Biology examples can be found in our 4MAT 4 Biology curriculum series, authors: Julia Koble and Joan Baltezore, 2009.)*

Teaching Strategy: Emotional impacting discussions

Use in Visual Art and the Media: As part of the lecture, students watch a five minute speeded up series of visual images from media sales promotions listing what had impact on them and why. Teacher follows with a discussion engaging the whole group.

The tinkerer manages with odds and ends...
None of the materials at the tinkerer's disposal has
a precise and definite function...
He modifies,retouches, adapts to new uses.

Francois Jacobs,[52] *1982*

Keep an eye out for the tinker shuffle, the flying
of kites, and kindred sources of surprise.

Bob Samples,[53] *1985*

Creating Quadrant Three: Collaborative Problem Solving

I love this word, *"tinkering."* So do today's learners. Think of their world, their social networks, the computer programs, the apps they use and create.

I saw an app recently, a credit card swipe that fits into the top of my iphone. If someone owes me money they can pay me with their credit card by swiping it over my phone. What a world this is for Type Three Learners!

The brain tinkers. Set up a tinkering laboratory in your classroom, a keen, exciting practicing and extending place where drills are not allowed and individuals and partners, and different size groups work collaboratively using lots of resources with multiple ways to practice.

Here are some tinkering examples from our biology course.

Question under study: How do cells regulate a balance between their internal and external environments?

> *Tinkering Task:* Create a cell to carry out a task.

Question under study: What does the statement, "You are what you eat." mean?

> *Tinkering Task:* Compare and contrast five fitness bars and make a decision on which would be the best for you.

Question under study: Why is there such a diversity of adaptations in life forms?

> *Tinkering Task:* Create a habitat game for an elementary classroom.

Start with the Big Ideas and your students will fill in (discover) the details and enjoy the doing of it. Research shows learning and remembering are linked to holding material in one's hands.[54]

Another Look at the Quadrant Three Parameters

The parameters that form Quadrant Three are *"thinking conceptually"* and *"acting on the learning."* This is where students take the lead. Understanding content at the conceptual level and acting on it in their own interest requires organized practice activities that present personal integration possibilities. Start with teacher structured practices that move students into tinkering and experimenting. This is designing for differentiation. The important details and specifics that fall under the concept umbrella must be included to be practiced and mastered in the options you give your students.

There is an empirical as well as a rational aspect to knowledge.

Immanuel Kant,[55] 1787

Theory can be learned only by practicing its application; its true knowledge lies in our ability to use it.

Alexandra Luria,[56] 1976

Motion is the context of living. We find meaning by and in our doing.

Robert Kegan,[57] 1998

Drill and testing is gone. Use interactive projects with intense feedback.

Riel Miller,[58] 2009

The goal is always that the learner takes over the learning. Think of that magic moment when your mentor let go of your bike and you took off.
That joyfulness is the magic of real learning.

Teaching Strategies for Quadrant Three

Learning is all in the using, never in rote memorizing. (It is literally not necessary; engagement cancels out the need for it.) Design problem solving projects for different groupings of students: individuals, partners, threesomes and so on. You want the students to gain real expertise from the practice you set up for them. The classroom needs to be as close to a laboratory as possible. Trying and trying again is honored. This is true in all content areas. Have exemplary examples of the tasks students can tackle. For example, freshmen in writing lab examining A papers written by seniors. Be available throughout all practice sessions, suggesting, supporting, challenging, remediating, moving around the classroom. This is exciting and real teaching.

Teaching Strategy: A drama performance

> *Use in Literature: To Kill a Mockingbird: A Readers Theatre* for a performance of the Tom Robinson trial including a script for Judge Taylor, Sheriff Tate, Atticus Finch, Mr.Gilmer, Bob Ewell and Mayella Ewell, Scout, Jem and Reverend Sykes with parts chosen and rehearsed by the students in sessions set by them as they prepare for a Quadrant Four performance with an audience to include outsiders.

Teaching Strategy: First drafting an original work

> *Use in Writing:* In a short story creative writing for the dialogue segment, students write an original story for the performance requirement. One of their practice tasks is to write a dialogue between an aloof really beautiful woman pumping her own gas and an attendant who wants to chat with her. She does not want to talk to him at all, but she needs to know how to get somewhere even though she doesn't want him to know she is lost.

To learn from experience is to make a backward and forward connection between what we do to things and what we enjoy or suffer from things inconsequence. Under such conditions, doing becomes a trying, an experiment with the world to find out what it is like; the undergoing becomes instruction–discovery of the connection of things.

John Dewey,[59] 1954

Teaching Strategy: Apply a math abstraction to real life

Use in Geometry: Teacher demonstrates with examples how the Pythagorean Theorem might be used to find the unknown side of a right angled triangle. Then the students must find a real life application and photograph it.*(Many of our Geometry examples can be found in our 4MAT 4 Geometry curriculum series, authors: Michael Arlien and Colleen Hodenfield, 2010.)*

Teaching Strategy: Competition for experiment success

Use in Chemistry: The students demonstrate improved methods of experimentally determining Absolute Zero, a contest between lab groups on eliminating error in determining Absolute Zero. The winning group explains the reason for their success.

Creating Quadrant Four Adaptations and Integration

What exactly do we teach that our students integrate into their lives, I mean really and truly use?

Think of this question every time you create an instructional design regarding your hoped-for learning results.Will this reading help my students know something that will help them in their lives? Will they use this mathematical function to problem solve? Will these skills help them to be able to communicate for their personal life needs?

Notice how the Learning Cycle returns students to new experiences, each one richer and more integrated. When you design your instruction to move students from experience to discovery you help them become more cognizant of their unique potential for originality. Life experiences that touch us stay with us. (Master teachers are themselves life experiences.)

We are not blank slates. All humans share similar sets of biases. Universal human nature is real. The trick is to understand what the universals are and how tightly or loosely they tie us down and to help our students know about them so they can embrace their ability to be original.

Shoppers will buy many more cans of soup if you put a sign atop the display that reads: *"Limit 12 per customer."*

How can you awake others to possibility and the
need for action in the name of possibility?
By opening spaces, clearings where people
can reach beyond where they are.

Maxine Greene,[60] *1996*

An innovation cannot be assimilated
unless its meaning is shared.

Michael Fullan,[61] *2007*

Another Look at the Quadrant Four Parameters

The parameters that form Quadrant Four are *"acting with the learning"* and *"integrating new learning."* This is the integration and transfer quadrant of the Learning Cycle. Students act on the learning and integrate it into their lives. This requires that the teacher offer doable options while mentoring, monitoring, and supporting them as they move to personal usefulness. As they complete each Learning Cycle, the students return to the experiential beginning of a new Cycle with more insight, deeper understanding and higher levels of expertise.

Teaching Strategies for Quadrant Four

In Quadrant Four, practice now becomes doing, and *the students are doing it for themselves.* The projects, the research, the art forms, the interviews, etc., all demanding and doable. The emphasis in planning Quadrant Four is on future possibilities. Students need to be convinced there are many things yet to be discovered in which they can take part; that there is growth and more expertise awaiting them in these new learnings. You are opening clearings for them.

Teaching Strategy: Creating an original poem

> *Use in Art: Primary:* Read *"My Family Lives Inside A Medicine Cabinet."* Students create original poem using their own family members and illustrate it.

Teaching Strategy: Political Cartoon

> *Use in Social Studies:* Students develop and present their point of view on a current issue and plan their own political cartoon. They must select an issue; decide on their message; sketch their idea, and write the punch line.

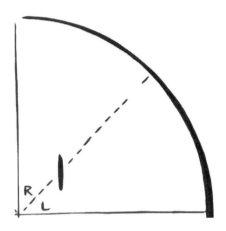

Feeling
Experiencing

R
L

Reflecting

Communication
Base

Valuing, Engaging
4MAT Base

Traveling the Complete Learning Cycle
The Four Competency-based Quadrants with Right- and Left-mode Strategies

Quadrant One – Communication

Connect: Quadrant One, Right Mode

Engage in and Reflect on Experience

The Quadrant One, Right-mode activity will…

> Connect learners directly to the concept experientially with enough impact to elicit sharing and discussion.

> Begin with a situation that is familiar to learners building on what they already know.

> Construct a learning experience that allows diverse and personal responses.

> Elicit authentic dialogue where idiosyncratic perceptions and reactions can be shared.

Attend: Quadrant One, Left Mode

Reflect and Analyze Experience

The Quadrant One, Left-Mode activity will…

> Guide learners to reflection and analysis of the experience.

> Draw learners into discussion to share diverse viewpoints and reactions.

> Summarize similarities and differences and establish a positive attitude toward the diversity of these reactions.

> Clarify the reason for the learning.

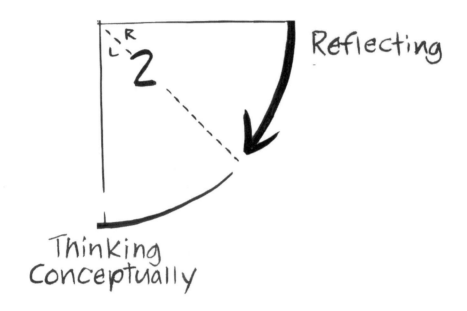

Reflecting

2

Thinking
Conceptually

Critical Thinking
Base

Understanding Expert Knowledge
4MAT Base

Quadrant Two – Critical Thinking

Image: Quadrant Two, Right Mode

See in Image and Metaphor and Conceptualize

A Quadrant Two, Right-Mode activity will…

Create a personal representation of the concept.

Use another medium to connect learners' personal knowing to the concept (visual, auditory, kinesthetic).

Provide a metaview, lifting learners into a wider view of the concept.

Deepen the connection between the concept and the learners' lives.

Inform: Quadrant Two, Left Mode

Learn theories and concepts

A Quadrant Two, Left-Mode activity will…

Take learners straight to the heart of the "acknowledged body of knowledge," the content.

Draw attention to important, discrete details, but not swamp learners with myriad facts.

Continually relate to the conceptual "Big Idea."

Use a variety of delivery systems: both teacher-directed and interactive lectures, Internet sources, texts, guest speakers, films, and demonstrations.

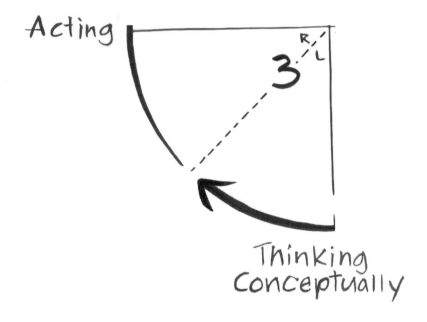

Acting

3 R L

Thinking
Conceptually

Collaborative
Problem Solving
Base

Becoming Skilled
4MAT Base

Quadrant Three – Collaborative Problem Solving

Practice: Quadrant Three, Left-Mode

Experiment and test "known" concepts and skills

A Quadrant Three, Left-Mode activity will…

Provide hands-on activities for practice and mastery in multiple ways (learning centers, games fostering skills development).

Check for understanding of concepts and skills using traditional worksheets, text problems, workbooks, and current multi media Internet online resources.

Set high expectations for skills mastery, determining with feedback if reteaching is necessary.

Provide opportunities for learners to create practice activities for each other.

Extend: Quadrant Three, Right- Mode

Explore new, original applications

A Quadrant Three, Right-Mode activity will…

Engage learners in collaborative real life problem-solving.

Create opportunities for learners to tinker and "mess" with the material, not practicing meaningless drills.

Offer as many creative options as possible so learners can design open-ended explorations of the learning and plan a unique "proof" of learning.

Require learners to begin the process of planning how their adaptations of the learning will be evaluated, identifying their criteria for excellence.

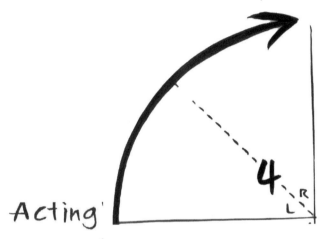

Creativity
Base

Adapting, Integrating
4MAT Base

Quadrant Four – Creativity

Refine: Quadrant Four, Left Mode

Analyze applications for relevance

A Quadrant 4, Left-Mode activity will…

Help learners analyze their use of the learning for relevance and originality.

Engage learners in editing and refining their work with the help of teacher and peers.

Give guidance and feedback, encouraging, assisting and suggesting refinements, turning mistakes into learning opportunities.

Maintain high expectations for completion of chosen options.

Perform: Quadrant Four, Right Mode

Share and celebrate learning

A Quadrant Four, Right-Mode activity will…

Establish a classroom atmosphere that celebrates all new learning, even failures.

Give learners the support they need to teach and share with others.

Make learner creations available to the larger community: their original books, their interview findings, their visuals, their demonstrations, the results of their experiments, their scientific findings of local environmental surveys, their illustrated family histories, and so on.

Leave learners intrigued by further possible applications of the concept, extending "What Ifs?" into future new learning.

Questions as We Travel the Learning Cycle

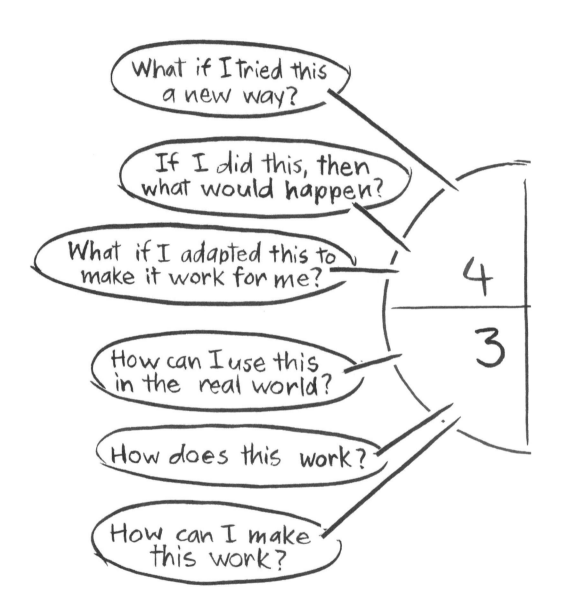

Questions as We Travel the Learning Cycle

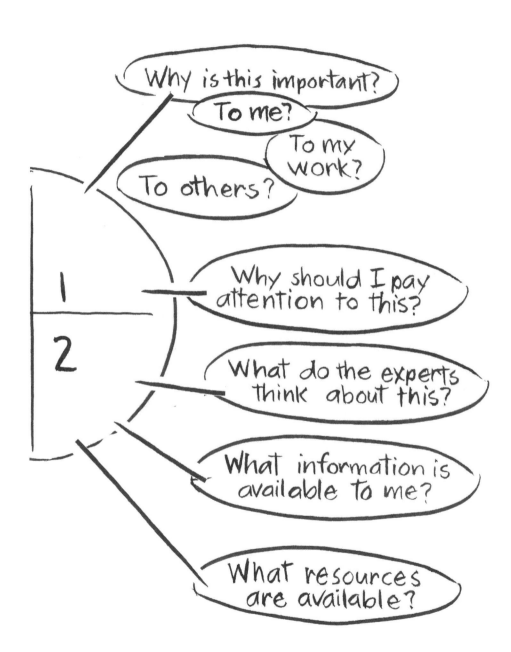

*We must find better ways to compete and
collaborate, to build a sustainable world
in an era of profound economic and
environmental interdependence.*

Ronald Heifetz et al[62], 2009

Two Important Aspects of Using the 4MAT Learning Cycle

What Will be Lost

Knowing exact outcomes

Maintaining your style of order

Losing control of your favorite content

Your status as the only teacher in the room

Working alone

Your cherished ideas about what every student must know

Awareness of What Will be Gained

Living comfortably with continuous emerging

More student diversity in response to learning tasks

Ability to help students develop the confidence to listen to their inner selves

A stronger experimental mind-set

A willingness to live with your losses

Working in collaborative teams most of the time

A shared language with fellow teachers who understand and use the Learning Cycle

Answer the Essential Question for Chapter Four

How can teachers master the flow around the Cycle?

5

Assessing Around
the Learning Cycle

Essential Question

*Why are multiple assessments necessary
in Learning Cycle instructional design?*

Assessment is about instruction,
because it can fundamentally transform
the way a teacher teaches.

W. James Popham,[63] *2008*

Teachers must explore the subtle nuances
of student development.
This is more complicated than grading,
it takes a more broader range of skills.

Bena Kalick,[64] *2009*

Assessing All the Way Around the Learning Cycle

"If you don't change assessment, nothing changes."

–Vito Perrone,[65] *2001*

This chapter reviews the larger conceptions of teaching the Learning Cycle design requires.

Assessment must be grounded in the knowledge of how people learn.

Assessment needs to include clear statements of what is important to learn.

Assessment needs to be flexible enough to meet the needs of a diverse student body.

Assessment must provide students with the opportunity to actively produce real work and demonstrate their knowing.

As your strategies and teaching techniques travel the cycle, you need to think about the different kinds of measurement you need as you move through the eight learning steps of the complete Cycle.

What differences in your assessments for

> meaning valuing,
>
> expert knowledge understandings,
>
> skills in the service of tinkering, experimenting and validating, and
>
> the multiple criteria you need for measuring performances.

What can be measured easily and what not so easily measured but of equal value?

For example, how will you measure mastery in calculating skills versus personal and authentic meaning in journal poetry entries?

These questions concern the evaluation of the whole child. Examine the chart on the next page.

The Learner...

Adapts learning
to personal life

Starts with personal meaning

Performs and
internalizes
learning

Is intrigued

Learner *Instructor*

adapts learning *creates meaning*
in a new way *and fascination*

Establishes
real-world
significance

Compares with
what is already
known

4 1

3 2

Applies
and
interprets

Creates a
mental
picture

Learner *Instructor*

masters skills and *develops key*
applies learning *concepts and*
knowledge

Tests theories

Investigates
naturally

Develops skills

Seeks out facts and knowledge

What the Student Does	What the Teacher Evaluates
Starts with personal meaning.	Requires judgment of tone and openness; Needs a trusting climate and empathy skills.
Is intrigued.	Accomplished only with hunch and the look of engagement in the student; not precise, but doable.
Compares with what is already known.	Yes, a task can be created for this.
Creates a mental picture.	Yes, if this ability has been taught to be made concrete in multiple ways.
Investigates naturally.	Experienced judgment on ease of flow; not precise, but doable.
Seeks out knowledge and facts.	Yes, can be measured.
Develops skills.	Yes, can be measured.
Tests theories.	Yes, can be measured.
Applies and interprets.	Yes, can be measured if specific, clear rubrics.
Establishes real-world significance.	Yes, can be measured if task is well structured.
Performs and internalizes learning.	Performs, yes; internalizes more vague unless questions require affect (feeling) answers.
Adapts learning to his/her life.	Yes, can be evaluated in both concrete and measurable ways if future requirements exist.

Many of these evaluations take more experience, use less accustomed tools, involve more complex judgments yet they are all important.

*Larger conceptions of teaching require
larger conceptions of evaluation.*

Vito Perrone, 2001

Dr. Perrone was right of course. The tasks that engage learners with a Cycle-designed plan involve the complete learning act, beginning with the learners themselves and if the design is conceptually cohesive, the beauty of the Cycle evolves, and the learner takes over the learning.

The Learning Cycle requires a larger conception of teaching and the most vital measure of success, that learners come to speak in their own voices.

A Voices Exercise

Remember back to a time in your life when you spoke up and it cost you. Go over the story in your own mind, or better yet tell it to a friend. Describe the courage it took for you to say what you had to say that day and describe what might have been or actually was the hardship that followed.

If you are having this conversation with a friend, ask for her or his story and listen well.

Then, take an opposite tack. Remember the details of a time, when you found yourself with someone or in a group where you were perfectly comfortable to speak in your own voice, to speak naturally with complete ease. What qualities were present in that situation where you could say what you meant and felt. Take a minute and jot down a few of what these qualities were.

When I do this activity in my workshops I always record the lists the different groups write on their charts to share with the larger group. Here are some of those qualities. Compare them with yours.

When I am perfectly comfortable in a group to be myself, to speak in my own voice...

> I feel supported.
>
> I feel listened to.
>
> I feel there is possibility to be even more open.
>
> I feel it is okay to be skeptical.
>
> I know it is okay to be wrong.
>
> Crazy ideas get shared, and we write them down.
>
> No one speaks on top of each other.
>
> I feel people honoring what I say.
>
> We all laugh a lot and sometimes cry.

How do we come to speak one day
in our own voice,
to dare a conversation
with the world?

Bernice McCarthy, 2000

When the small groups hold up their lists of qualities, they are remarkably alike. It seems we all have the same experiences of the ambience that enables us to speak in our own voices.

These are the qualities of a *perfect* classroom climate! Go back and read them again.

When we understand this we can see how assessment functions in a master teacher's classroom. It is open, it is comfortable, it is authentic, it goes on all the time and students grow.

How Voices Differ as You Move Around the Cycle

The first voice is the student's own as they share their observations. Then the sharing of perceptions enlarges the voices to include fellow students. The sharing is followed by images the students create to clarify the meaning of their own perceptions. These three steps on the cycle are where students are in dialogue with themselves and each other.

Then the teacher's voice takes precedence. S/he speaks with the combined voices of the experts while the students record, interpret and even question the meaning of the expert voices.

Then the students practice in the way of the experts, their voices still more muted as they grasp the expert meanings.

Then in the final and culminating steps of The Learning Cycle, the students now speak in their own cvoices blending the learning into an adaptation, integration and oftentimes performance of the learning.

Children have two visions,
the inner and the outer.
Of the two,
the inner vision is brighter.

Sylvia Ashton Warner,[66] *1963*

What is assessment after all but sitting beside to judge together?

> *Assessment is a conversation;*
> *a conversation that takes place*
> *first, within me as I come into the world,*
> *with my mother, father, my siblings,*
> *then with others as we begin to share our worlds,*
> *then between my teachers and me as I learn the*
> *world of the experts,*
> *and finally between me and my work.*
> *This final conversation ultimately becomes the one*
> *I have on a continuing basis with the world.*

External and internal criteria. Do I balance my listening by attending to both voices?
What do they say about my progress?
What do I think and feel about my progress?

Clearly, I cannot have this conversation if I never learn to speak in my own voice.

This melding of internal and external criteria is the heart of true growth as we come more and more to trust our own voices and far better able to understand and critique the voices of others.

As we grow and mature, we listen differently to the experts. We ponder and wonder about what they tell us more than we did when we were younger. But our own voice grows stronger. The balance we now bring to our inner voice and the attention we pay to external voices is the path that leads to wisdom.

Assess: To sit beside and judge.

Examine how the learner's roles change as they move around the Cycle: from connecting to reflecting, to imaging the concept, to understanding the knowledge base, to practicing, to experimenting, to editing and polishing, and to performance – their own best critic.

Then they have their own voice.

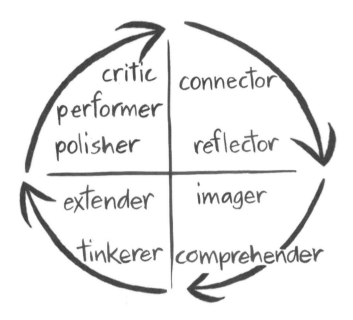

Two Kinds of Criteria

Assessment is the process of gathering, describing or quantifying information about performance.

There are two kinds of criteria:

> *internal* (one's self), and

> *external* (the experts).

We need to invite the conversation between the two.

The word assessment means literally to sit beside. This is the immutable image one needs to have in order to do this well; teacher and student in meaningful conversation.

On the Way   **At the Gate**

On-the-Way or At-the-Gate or Both

Examine how the Learning Cycle requires both formative and summative assessments with an emphasis on final performance and integration.

We need to assess how they are doing in the learning as well as what they have learned. We need to be more concerned with the video playing out in their growth and development than the test result snap-shots we gather.

On-the-Way and At-the-Gate Assessments

Put a check mark on the items below from both columns of this balance sheet to see how many of these two kinds of assessments you use.

On the Way – To Form	At the Gate – To Sum
to perfect a process	to measure what was done
method is description	method is measurement
qualitative	quantitative
ongoing reaction to treatment with an eye to developing it	Did we do what we tried to do?
data for growth and change, checkpoints for adaptations, goal-setting while you're doing it	data for reporting decisions, what's been learned, leads to goal-setting for the next time
Where are you in the learning of this?	What did you learn?
developmental	completion oriented
ongoing – a video	at certain times – a snapshot
"ing" – How are we doing?	"ed" – What happened?

Assessment done properly should
begin conversations about performance,
not end them.

Bernice McCarthy, 2000

Oftentimes, teachers will suggest that we need very few At-the-Gate assessments in elementary school. Rather we need to be primarily concerned with how students are doing developmentally.

While I know we need the balance of both, I also understand that gates are very good things.

Imagine that you are learning to play the cello. You would not be very skilled at first. Your teacher would be monitoring your On-the-Way development. But in due time when you ask to be the "First Chair" in the cello section, only high expectations and rigorous training will make that possible. That would be a major Gate and a worthy goal.

Yet each Gate a student passes through leads to a more vigorous On-the-Way. And so it repeats. This entire Learning Cycle is an elegant movement from novice to aficionado to virtuoso.

On the next page examine the list and try differentiating your ideas of On-the-Way and At-the-Gate tasks. Draw a line from each task over toward the image you think it matches. If you think it might be some of one and some of the other, draw short lines, if it is all one or the other draw longer lines.

After you have finished, ask yourself, "Does it depend on my purpose?"

If yes, what kinds of purposes would change your decisions?

On the Way

At the Gate

a demonstration

a journal

an essay

a term paper

a diorama

a poster

a student-created skit

a mindmap

a group discussion

a quiz

an outline

a 3-dimensional model

an interview

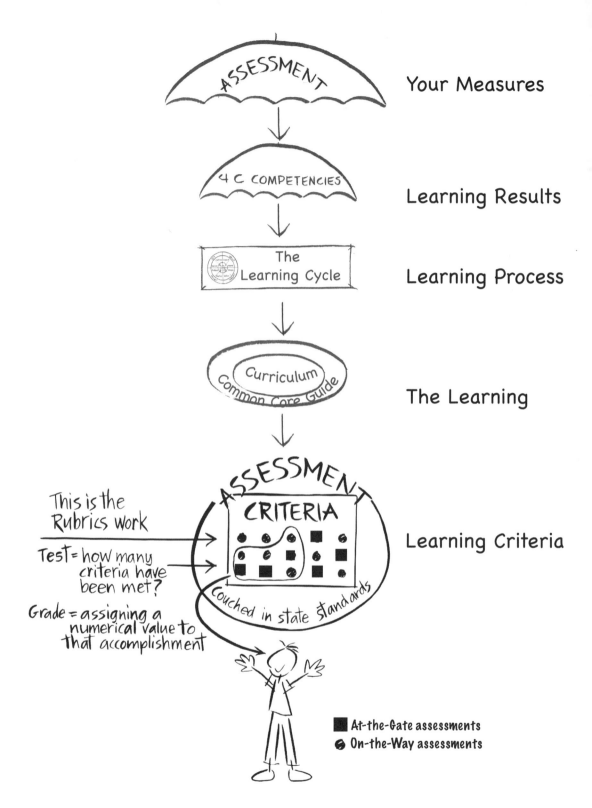

ASSESSMENT — Your Measures

4 C COMPETENCIES — Learning Results

The Learning Cycle — Learning Process

Curriculum
Common Core Guide — The Learning

ASSESSMENT
CRITERIA — Learning Criteria

This is the Rubrics work

Test = how many criteria have been met?

Grade = assigning a numerical value to that accomplishment

Couched in state standards

■ At-the-Gate assessments
◕ On-the-Way assessments

The Visual for a Complete Assessment Package

Concept Choices: the top umbrella is your assessment package based on your content and your students and your concept choices.

Learning Results: the second umbrella symbolizes your resulting investment in the 4 competencies, how you are focusing on their inclusion as the major goal of your intended learning results.

The Process: The rectangle below that (the Bridge) is the process you will use to create your instructional design and its correlating assessment package.

The Learning: Your curriculum is represented by the double oval, as is guided by the common core standards.

The Criteria: the criteria represents what you have chosen to measure for your learning results and includes both On-the-Way and At-the-Gate measures. It is the rubrics that clarify your expectations. As often as possible it is a powerful strategy to create it with the students.

The Learner will be awarded a grade. The grade will be the number of criteria of both kinds of assessment, On-the-Way and At-the-Gate, that make the equivalent of an A or a B and so on, determined with a constantly focused eye on you district/state standards.

The Formula for a Complete Assessment Package

Continually examine the outcome relationship to the 4 Competencies.

Decide on your outcomes based on your conceptualized content.

Create the criteria that must be present for the learning results you want.

Decide on how that will be measured, engage the students in this.

Use a balance of both On-the Way and At-the Gate measures.

Develop a scoring system.

Validate it with exemplary examples. (Remember my example of how I used "A" papers from a respected teacher of senior students as examples for my sophomores in my creative writing classes.) There are many more possibilities like this.

The Final Learning Cycle Design Step:
Adding Your Assessments

Assessment Quadrant One

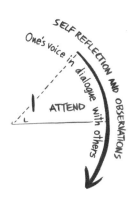

Active listening, dialogue and reflection

Has the student been an active contributor to the group?

Has the student listened?

Has the student assimilated and reflected upon the feelings/thoughts of the other group members?

Has the student expressed his feelings and thoughts?

Has the dialogue helped the student to better understand her position?

Communication Competency: Quadrant One – Meaning

connecting   experiencing   collaborating

discussing   assuming roles   relating to personally

journaling   brainstorming   imagining

hunching   sharing   empathizing

responding   listening   questioning

Assessment Quadrant Two

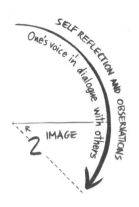

Concept Congruence

Are the students' concept images as presented visually, auditorially and kinesthetically congruent (corresponding) with those of the experts, those the teacher is aiming for?

Do the concept presentations indicate understanding and individuality of thought regarding the big idea experienced in Quadrant One?

Knowledge clarity

Do the students understand the material conceptually? In other words, do they see the big picture, how the parts connect, how the facts relate to the issues?

Do the students see the relationships of the content to real life?

Have they mastered the essentials, the essence of the material?

Critical Thinking Competency: Quadrant Two – Image and Ideas

becoming informed	*defining*	*understanding*
explaining	*identifying*	*analyzing*
categorizing	*imaging*	*patterning*
sequencing	*knowing*	*relating to other*
conceptualizing	*recognizing*	*picturing*
listing	*classifying*	*checking evidence*

Assessment Quadrant Three

Skills necessary to proceed

Has the practice required of the students enabled them to use the material skillfully?

Can they now take what they have learned and place it in the context of their lives?

Collaborative Problem Solving Competency: Quadrant Three – Skills

practicing	*using*	*tinkering*
synthesizing	*locating*	*measuring*
experimenting	*editing*	*interpreting*
reconstructing	*debating*	*commenting*
paraphrasing	*arranging in chronological order*	*comparing*
adjusting	*opening to emergence*	*deciding doability*

Performance Assessment

Has the student used higher order skills in combination with content to:

solve an interesting problem?

present an overview of the material?

raise questions that lead to further study, with originality and flair, acknowledging all sources?

Creative Competency: Quadrant Four – Adaptations

merging	creating	re-presenting
adapting	developing	illustrating-verbally
illustrating	nonverbally	exploring
expanding	performing	polishing
sharing	elaborating	synthesizing
extending	making	questioning anew

This plea for help was on a piece of scrap paper left inside a standardized test booklet in math. It was discovered by the teacher after the booklets were collected. The child was a first grade student. A dragon—something to think about.

A Final Thought on Foreseeing 21ˢᵗ Century Learning Results

Communication: Web-site learning communities will form with student authors and their peers reaching out to the larger world.

Critical Thinking: Teaching will become more and more a designing function to include customized knowledge areas, with both fluid analysis and synthesizing abilities in addition to functional technologies not yet imagined.

Collaborative Problem Solving: Higher education learning communities will proliferate where students use high-speed mobile devices to connect to large databases. Learning interactions would be with many teachers, some thousands of miles away, working on the same issues.

Creativity: Teachers will be coaching students through original adaptations of their learning. It requires deep and competent understanding of content and its interdisciplinary ramifications. Coaching needs a research-oriented mind, and the ability to be open to students just the way they are, coupled with a passion for and a vision of what they are becoming. Coaching excellence is no small task.

Are our young teachers being prepared for this?

Answer the Essential Question for Chapter Five

Why are multiple assessments necessary in Learning Cycle instructional design?

6

The Endurance and Continuity of the Learning Cycle

Essential Question

Is the Learning Cycle the key to education in the 21st Century?

There is nothing so practical as a good theory.

Kurt Lewin,[67] 1951

There is nothing wiser than the circle.

Rainer Maria Rilke,[68] 2005

These are the major experiential learning theorists that form the base of The Learning Cycle. They are well known in the field of pedagogy.

Lev Vygotsky[69]: Soviet cognitive scientist. *Zone of Proximal Development* (1947)

> Learning from experience is the process whereby human development occurs in confrontation with the dialectic conflicts inherent in experiential learning, that is, using dialogue to stimulate reflection and action on the world in order to transform it. Learning occurs in communication with others when we problem solve in collaboration with more capable peers.

Vygotsky was Influenced by Jean Piaget, Kurt Lewin and others.

John Dewey: American philosopher, psychologist and educational reformer speaking about what changes we need to transform education (1938)

> There are certain common principles in the new education. from imposition from above to expression and cultivation of individuality, from external discipline to free activity, from learning from texts and teachers, to learning from experience, from acquisition of isolated skills and techniques by drill to acquisition as means of attaining ends which make direct vital appeal, from preparation for a more or less remote future to making the most of the opportunities of present life, from static aims and materials to acquaintance with a changing world.

Dewey maintained that if learning is real, it creates purpose and direction leading to change, then on to transformation. He illustrated this premise with a cycle.

Observing,

then connecting what we experience,

then gaining new knowledge,

and judging that knowledge in relation to what we already know,

then acting with purpose,

finally integrating new learning into our lives.

The Cycle repeats.

"When intellectual experience and its material are taken to be primary, the cord that binds nature and experience is cut."

–*John Dewey*

...thinking is not only intentional,
it is also necessarily fraught with the roots
that it embodies. It has a from-to structure.

We can know more than we can tell.

Michael Polanyi,[70] 1967

Kurt Lewin: Founder of American Social Psychology (1947)

> The integration of theory and practice. Learning is best facilitated in an environment where there is dialectic tension between immediate experience and analytic detachment...This emphasis on subjective experience has developed into a strong commitment in the practice of experiential learning to values of personal involvement and responsibility...emphasizing that feelings as well as thoughts are facts.
> *Lewin created the original Cycle.*

Jean Piaget[71]: French Developmental Psychologist (1929)

> Intelligence is shaped by experience, not an innate characteristic but a product of the interaction between the person and the environment. Action is the key. The ability to abstract and conceptualize happens when we act in exploring the immediate concrete environment.

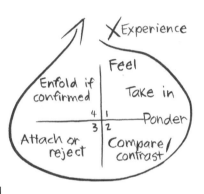

We feel it, are taken in by it, ponder it, compare and contrast it, attach or reject it, enfold it if it confirms.

This calls us to do two things: to continue to believe in our experience, enriching and deepening our confirmed knowings, and second, to open to new things, even if they may confound our previous knowing.
The Cycle repeats.

Michael Polanyi: Philosopher of Science and Social Science: *The Tacit Dimension* (1967)

> Creative acts, especially discovery, are charged with strong personal feelings and commitments He argued that science is not value-free, it abounds often with informed guesses, hunches and imaginings that are exploratory and motivated by passions.

> Tacit knowledge is pre-logical and includes a range of conceptual and sensory information and images that can be brought to bear in an attempt to make sense of something. This inevitably leads to discovery.

> From ourselves, to interiorizing, to understanding, to using the newness.
> *The Cycle repeats.*

Without the interplay between emotion and logic there is no knowledge. Human growth is a diversity of human formations.

David Kolb,[72] 1982

Alfred North Whitehead[73]: English mathematician and philosopher (1967)

Whitehead has a cycle for three "periods" in education the freedom stage, the discipline stage and the generalization stage.

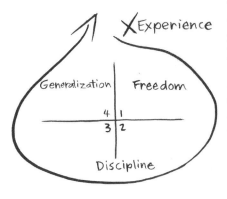

Freedom: the student must choose to be interested and want to move to the process of becoming, being filled with wonder with a freedom that allows the learner to see with independent choices.

Discipline: the development of best practice, examining data, learning facts, concentrating with purpose.

Generalization: when something is known and apprehended, shedding details in favor of application of principles. This is real learning, now invested in possibilities.
The Cycle repeats.

David Kolb: American educational theorist: Learning Styles Theorist (1982)

David Kolb and his generous personal help over the years has been the foundation of my work on the Learning Cycle. Kolb maintains that the ideal learning process engages all four of these learning modes in response to situational demands. As individuals begin to use all four approaches, they tend to develop strengths in one perceiving approach and one processing approach forming a penchant for one or two styles over the others. For effective learning, people need all four. People need to travel the Cycle.

The Ones strengths are valuing skills

The Twos strengths are thinking skills

The Threes strengths are decision making skills.

The Fours strengths are acting skills.

Clearly, we need expertise in all four. *The Cycle repeats.*

"Learning is the creation of knowledge through the transformation of experience."

–David Kolb

*The core capacity needed to access
the field of the future is presence.
Deep listening, being open
beyond one's preconceptions...
letting go of old identities and the
need for control and making choices
to serve the evolution of life.*

Peter Senge et al.,[74] 2004

Arthur E. Wise[75]: President emeritus of the National Council for Accreditation of Teacher Education (2012)

> *"The primary force resisting change is right in front of us. Eventually, reformers of nearly every stripe—conservative, progressive, managerial, professional, or technological—hit the wall they do not see: the wall that surrounds every classroom. Time and again, reform plans do not reform, much less transform.*
>
> *The cause is simple: the 19th-century 'egg crate' school and its key design feature, a self-contained, four-walled classroom with a fully qualified teacher for every 25 or so students (well, maybe 30 or 35, or even more in hard times).*
>
> *Continued and rigid adherence to this design reinforces the status quo, making it a tyrannical force against change."*

Examine these four key attributes of the Millennials and contrast them with Dr. Wise's statement of why reform has not worked in our schools.

Four Key Millennial Attributes

> Networking, belief in inclusion
>
> Unlimited access to knowledge and information
>
> Commitment to stewardship and collaborative problem solving
>
> Belief they can create and innovate

These things do not get done with students working individually on skills and drills. These things do not get done in lecture-heavy classrooms and auditoriums. These things do not get done without real world problems to collaborate on. These things do not get done without the resources and opportunities for original, far-flung open-ended learning projects, accompanied by teacher-student co-created rubrics.

We know how learning works. We have known for some time.

Answer the Essential Question for Chapter Six

Is the Learning Cycle the key to education in the 21st Century?

Endnotes
and
Index

Endnotes

1. Fullan, Michael, (2003). *The Moral Imperative of School Leadership.* Thousand Oaks, CA: Corwin Press.

2. Partnership for 21st Century Skills, *http://www.p21.org*

3. Hammond, Linda-Darling, (2010). *The Flat World and Education: How America's Commitment to Equity Will Determine Our Future.* Columbia: Teacher's College Press.

4. Shlain,Tiffany, (2011). Interview on *dailydot.com*

5. Pew Research, (2011), *http://pewresearch.org/millenials*

6. Winogras, Morley and Michael D. Hais, (2011). *Millennial Momentum.* New Jersey: Rutgers Univ Press.

7. Beloit College Mind-Set List for the Class of 2015, *http://www.beloit.edu/mindset*

8. Neif, Ron. Emeritus director of public affairs at Beloit College

9. Howe, Neil and William Strauss, (2007). *Millennials Go to College.* Paramount Market Publishing.

10. Page, Larry, *http://www.google.com/about/company/tech.html*

11. Zull, James E., (2002). *The Art of Changing the Brain: Enriching the Practice of Teaching and Exploring the Biology of Learning.* Sterling, Va; Stylus Press.

12. Kegan, Robert, (1982). *The Evolving Self: Problem and Progress in Human Development.* Cambridge, MA: Harvard University Press.

13. Hellige, Joseph B., (2001). *Hemispheric Asymmetry: What's Right and What's Left.* Cambridge, MA: Harvard University Press.

14. Sperry, Roger. *http://www.nobelprize.org/nobel_prizes/medicine/laureates/1981/sperry-lecture.html*

15. Kahneman, Daniel, (2011). *Thinking, Fast and Slow.* New York: Farrar, Straus, Giroux.

16. Heath, Chip and Dan Heath, (2010). *Switch: How to Change Things When Change is Hard.* New York: Broadway Books.

17. McGilchrist, Iain, (2009). *The Master and His Emissary: The Divided Brain and the Making of the Western World.* New Haven, CT: Yale University Press.

18. Orstein, Robert, (1997). *The Right Mind: Making Sense of the Hemispheres.* NY: Harcourt Brace.

19. Bateson, Mary Catherine, (1994). *Peripheral Visions.* New York: Harper Collins.

20. Benson, D. Frank, (1985). "Left-Hemisphere Language" in *The Dual Brain.* New York: Guilford Press.

21. Singapore Primary Math (2001), *http://www.singaporemath.com/Singapore_Math_Story_s/10.htm*

22. Armstrong, Karen, (2009). *The Case for God.* New York: Anchor Books.

23. Goldberg, Elkhonon, (2009). *The Executive Brain.* USA: Oxford University Press.

24. Sanders, Judith and Donald Sanders, (1984). *Teaching Creativity Through Metaphor: An Integrated Brain Approach.* New York: Longmans.

25. de Man, Paul, (1984). *The Rhetoric of Romanticism.* NY: Columbia University Press.

26. Sathian, Krish. *http://www.eurekalert.org/pub_releases/2012-02/eu-hma020312.php*

27. Zull, James E., (2011). *From Brain to Mind: Using Neuroscience to Guide Change in Education.* Sterling, Va; Stylus Press.

28. McCarthy, Bernice. (2000) *About Teaching.* Wauconda, IL: About Learning Publishing.

29. Gelb, Michael, K. Howell and T. Buzaan, (2011). *Brain Power: Improve Your Mind as You Age.* New World Library, newworldlibrary.com

30. Whyte, David, (2002). *The Heart Aroused: Poetry and the Preservation of the Soul in Corporate America.* New York: Doubleday.

31. Damasio, Antonio, (2003). *Looking for Spinoza: Joy Sorrow, and the Feeling Brain.* New York: Harcourt

32. Feynman, Richard. (1969) "What is Science?", 15th Annual National Science Teachers Association, in New York City (1966) published in The Physics Teacher Vol. 7, issue 6

33. Whitehead, Alfred North. (2001) Dialogues of Alfred North Whitehead. Godine.com, David R. Godine.

34. Roschellel, Jeremy and Stephanie D. Teasley, (1995). *Collaborative Problem Solving.*

35. Robinson, Sir Ken, (2006). *TED, http://www.ted.com*

36. Hunt, David E., (1987). *Beginning With Ourselves: In Practice, Theory and Human Affairs.* Cambridge, MA: Brookline Books

37. Goodlad, John, (1984). *A Place Called School.* New York: McGraw Hill, 20th Anniversary Ed., 2004.

38. Rutherford, James, (1991). *Science for All Americans.* New York, Oxford University Press.

39. Dewey, John, (1954, reprinted, 1980). *Art as Experience.* New York: Perigee Books.

40. *www.corestandards.org*

41. Sawyer, Robert Keith. (2006). *The Cambridge Handbook of the Learning Sciences.* New York: Cambridge University Press.

42. Holmes, Oliver Wendell, *http://en.wikiquote.org/wiki/Talk:Oliver_Wendell_Holmes,_Jr*

43. Bateson, Mary Catherine, *ibid.*

44. McGilchrist,Iain. *ibid.*

45. Carey, Ken, (1991). *The Third Millennium: Living in the Posthistoric World.* New York: Harper One.

46. Kolb, David A, (1984). *Experiential Learning: Experience as the Source of Learning and Development.* Englewood Cliffs NJ: Prentice-Hall.

47. Meyer, Dan, appeared on TED speaking about teaching math. *http://blog.mrmeyer.com*

48. Elmore, Richard, (2004). *School Reform From the Inside Out: Policy, Practice and Performance.* Cambridge, MA: Harvard University Press.

49. Nelson, George. Former director of Project 2061 and a member of the senior staff of the American Association for the Advancement of Science.

50. Alberts, Bruce. Editor-in-Chief, Science, Professor Emeritus in biochemistry and biophysics, University of California, San Francisco, formerly President of the National Academy of Sciences.

51. Piaget, Jean, (1929, reprint 1951). *The Child's Conception of the World.* Savage: MD Littlefield Adams

52. Jacob, Francois. "Evolutionary tinkering with transposable elements." *http://www.pnas.org/content/103/21/7941.short*

53. Samples, Bob, Bill Hammond, Bernice McCarthy. (1985) *4MAT and Science: Toward Wholeness in Science Education.* Barrington, IL: Excel, Inc.

54. Hands, gestures research *http://www.sciencedaily.com/re-leases/2007/07/070725105957.htm*

55. Kant, Immanuel, (1787). *The Critique of Pure Reason.* Trans. Werner Pluhar. Indianapolis: Hackett, 1996.

56. Luria, Alexandra, (1976). *The Working Brain: An Introduction to Neuropsychology.* New York: Basic Books.

57. Miller, Riel, *http://www.rielmiller.com*

58. Kegan, Robert. *ibid.*

59. Dewey, John, (1938). *Experience and Education.* Kappa Delta Pi.

60. Greene, Maxine, (1996). "In Search of a Critical Pedagogy," in *Breaking Free: The Transformative Power of Critical Pedagogy.* Pepi Leistyna, A.Woodrum, S. Sherblom Eds. Cambridge, MA: Harvard Educational Review.

61. Fullan, Michael, (2007). *The New Meaning of Educational Change, 4th Ed.* New York: Teachers College Press.

62. Heifetz, Ronald, A Grashow, M. Linsky, (2009). *The Practice of Adaptive Leadership: Tools and Tactics for Changing Your Organization and the World.* Cambridge, MA: Harvard Business Press.

63. Popham, W. James, (2008). *Transformative Assessment.* Alexandria, VA: ASCD.

64. Kalick, Bena. and A. Costa, (2009). *Habits of Mind Across the Curriculum: Practical and Creative Strategies for Teachers.* Alexandria, VA. ASCD.

65. Perrone, Vito. Director of the Teacher Education Program, Harvard School of Education.

66. Warner, Sylvia Ashton, (1963). *Teacher.* New York,Touchstone.

67. Lewin, Kurt, (1951). *Field Theory in Social Sciences.* New York: Harper and Row.

68. Rilke, Maria Rainer, (2005). *The Poet's Guide to Life: The Wisdom of Rilke.* Trans. E. Baer. NY: Modern

69. Vygotsky, Lev, (1934, 1986). *Thought and Language.* Cambridge, MA: MIT Press.

70. Polyani, Michael, (1966-1983). *The Tacit Dimension.* Gloucester, MA: Peter Smith.

71. Piaget, Jean, *ibid.*

72. Kolb, David A., *ibid.*

73. Whitehead, Alfred North, (1929). *Aims of Education and Other Essays.* New York: Macmillan ISBN: ISBN-10: 0029351804

74. Senge, Peter et al., (2004). *Presence: An Exploration of Profound Change in People Organizations, and Society.* New York: Doubleday. ISBN: 0-385-517624-x

75. Wise, Arthur, E., (2012). *Education Week,* January 25, 2012 *http://tinyurl.com/89b9aq3*

Index

Refine, 41, 57, 137

A

Abrahams, Frank, 113

al Abdullah, Queen Rania of Jordan, 1

Alberts, Bruce, 120

Armstrong, Karen, 44

Ashdown, Paddy, 1

Assessment, ii-iii, 143-174
  Voices Exercise, 149

  Assessing All the Way Around the Learning Cycle, 143

  At-the-Gate, ii, 157, 161

  How Voices Move Around the Cycle, 151

  On-the-Way, ii, 157, 161

  The Formula, 163

  Two Kinds of Criteria, 155

  What the Student Does, 147

  What the Teacher Evaluates, 147

  Adding Assessments Around the Cycle, 165-171

21st century, i, ii, iii, 1, 7, 13, 17, 61, 85, 97, 103, 105, 173, 175, 183

4 Cs, i, 81, 162-163
  Collaborative Problem Solving, i, 23, 51, 63, 73, 75, 99, 123, 134-135, 162, 169, 173

  Communication, i, 1, 19, 51, 63, 65, 67, 107, 109, 130-131, 162, 165, 173

  competencies, i, ii, 1, 13, 61-63, 69, 71-77, 99, 101

  Creativity, i, 1, 25, 63, 77-79, 99, 136-137, 162, 171-173

    Critical Thinking i, 1, 21, 49, 51, 53, 63, 69-71, 117, 132-133, 153, 159, 162, 167, 173

4MAT Learning Cycle, 15, 63, 69-81, 95-98, 141

4MAT Model, iii, 40, 67, 71, 75, 79

  Attend, 41, 131

  Connect, 41, 59, 131

  Extend, 41, 135

  Image, 39, 41, 133

  Inform, 41, 133

  Perform, 41, 137

  Practice, 39, 41, 73, 123-125, 135

B

Bateson, Mary Catherine, 38, 106

Beloit College Mind-Set List for the Class of 2015, 9

Benson, D. Frank, 39, 68

best practices, 37

bridge, 85-93
  outcomes imaged, 85-93

C

Carey, Ken, 112

Common Core Standards, ii, 95-101
  Examples from, 95-101

Concepts, ii, 39, 41, 53, 61, 68-69, 81-101, 109-113, 131, 133, 137

  6 Trick, 92-95

  Concept Characteristics, 83

  Concept/Content Umbrella, 84-95

  Conceptualize Their Content, 85-91

Content, 13, 61, 69, 71, 81-101, 111-119, 133, 141, 173

Core of the Instructional Design, 81